Juvenile Delinquency
and Delinquents

MASTERS SERIES IN CRIMINOLOGY

Series Editor
Henry N. Pontell
School of Social Ecology, University of California, Irvine

White-Collar and Corporate Crime
by Gilbert Geis

Electronic Crime
by Peter Grabosky

Chasing After Street Gangs: A Forty-Year Journey
by Malcolm W. Klein

Juvenile Delinquency and Delinquents: The Nexus of Social Change
by James F. Short, Jr. and Lorine A. Hughes

FORTHCOMING

Feminist Criminology: Crime, Patriarchy, and the Control of Women
by Meda Chesney-Lind

The Great Punishment Experiment
by Todd R. Clear

Social Support and Crime in America: A New Criminology
by Francis T. Cullen

Social Roots of Crime: Why Some Societies Are More Violent Than Others
by Elliott Currie

Developmental and Life Course Theories of Offending
by David P. Farrington

Crimes of Memory
by Elizabeth Loftus

Identity Fraud
by Henry N. Pontell

**MASTERS SERIES
IN CRIMINOLOGY**

James F. Short, Jr. and Lorine A. Hughes

Juvenile Delinquency and Delinquents: The Nexus of Social Change

PEARSON
Prentice
Hall

UPPER SADDLE RIVER, NEW JERSEY
COLUMBUS, OHIO

To our mentors, colleagues, and students

Library of Congress Cataloging-in-Publication Data

Short, James F., Jr.
 Juvenile delinquency and delinquents : the nexus of social change / James F. Short, Jr. and Lorine A. Hughes. — 1st ed.
   p. cm.
 Includes bibliographical references and index.
 ISBN-13: 978-0-13-512737-7 (alk. paper)
 ISBN-10: 0-13-512737-8 (alk. paper)
 1. Juvenile delinquency. 2. Social work with juvenile delinquents. 3. Juvenile justice, Administration of. I. Hughes, Lorine A., II. Title.
 HV9069.S537 2008
 364.36—dc22

2007040765

Editor-in-Chief: Vernon R. Anthony
Senior Acquisitions Editor: Tim Peyton
Editorial Assistant: Alicia Kelly
Marketing Manager: Adam Kloza
Senior Marketing Coordinator: Alicia Dysert
Production Manager: Joanne Riker
Cover Design Director: Jayne Conte
Cover Design: Brian Kane
Full-Service Project Management/Composition: Integra Software Services, Ltd.
Printer/Binder: Courier Companies, Inc.

Credits and acknowledgments borrowed from other sources and reproduced, with permission, in this textbook appear on appropriate page within text.

Copyright © 2008 by Pearson Education, Inc., Upper Saddle River, New Jersey, 07458. All rights reserved. Printed in the United States of America. This publication is protected by Copyright and permission should be obtained from the publisher prior to any prohibited reproduction, storage in a retrieval system, or transmission in any form or by any means, electronic, mechanical, photocopying, recording, or likewise. For information regarding permission(s), write to: Rights and Permissions Department.

Pearson Education LTD.
Pearson Education Australia PTY, Limited
Pearson Education Singapore, Pte. Ltd
Pearson Education North Asia Ltd
Pearson Education, Canada, Ltd
Pearson Educación de Mexico, S.A. de C.V.
Pearson Education–Japan
Pearson Education Malaysia, Pte. Ltd

PEARSON
Prentice
Hall

10 9 8 7 6 5 4 3 2 1
ISBN-13: 978-0-13-512737-7
ISBN-10:   0-13-512737-8

CONTENTS

Preface   vii

CHAPTER 1   The Discovery of Childhood and Its Consequences   1

CHAPTER 2   The Continuing Evolution of the Juvenile Court System and Its Consequences   19

CHAPTER 3   Studying Juvenile Delinquency and Juvenile Delinquents   39

CHAPTER 4   The Social Distribution of Delinquency and Delinquents   49

CHAPTER 5   Explaining Juvenile Delinquency and Delinquents   77

CHAPTER 6   Systems of Control and the Socialization of Children   107

CHAPTER 7   What Is The World Coming To? (And What Does It Have To Do With Juvenile Delinquency?)   127

References   137

Bibliography   142

Index   147

PREFACE

When Henry Pontell inquired about my participation in this series, I agreed to think about it but put off a decision for more than a year. Lorine A. Hughes (Lori) and I were working on new analyses of the Chicago street gang data that were the basis for her dissertation, and that was my first priority. Lori soon became a partner in other projects and I realized that her co-authorship was necessary if I were to undertake this project as well. I am grateful to Henry and to the publisher for their agreement to make Lori a full partner in the enterprise.

The "jumping off" point of the book is *Delinquency and Society*, my book in the Prentice Hall Foundations of Modern Sociology Series (Short, 1990). Readers of that book will find many similarities with this one. This book is both more and less than that one; less because it is not as comprehensive in its treatment of some topics, more because recent statistical data and scholarship are included. Space constraints and an effort to make accessible to a general audience the study of delinquency and of delinquents result in differences in style of presentation. It is more as well because control of delinquency and what to do about delinquents are discussed, albeit very briefly. And it is more—at least different—because the customary constraints and cautions that we exercise in scholarly, and particularly scientific, exegesis have been loosened somewhat in order to facilitate communication with younger generations which inevitably must cope with these problems. Finally, the book is more, and certainly better, because it is a collaborative effort with Lori Hughes, a much younger "master" than I.

James F. Short, Jr.

1 | THE DISCOVERY OF CHILDHOOD AND ITS CONSEQUENCES

It is not for history to supply us with a sense of history. Life always supplies us with a sense of history. It is for history to supply us with a sense of life.

Adam Gopnik (2006a, p. 84)

History tells us that many things we take for granted (because they are so much a part of our experience) have not always been as we experience and believe them to be. If we want to understand or change them, therefore, it is useful to examine how they came to be as they are. Ask anyone what juvenile delinquency is, for example, and the response is likely to be that it is illegal behavior committed by young people. It is that, but it is much more. At least some of the behavior that is called juvenile delinquency is as old as human history—parents and other adults have probably always complained of the shortcomings of the young—but much is also new. Even the *idea* of juvenile delinquency is relatively new, reflecting changing beliefs and understandings about children and families and communities. So why not begin with what it is all about today? There are in fact several reasons for not doing that:

- Juvenile *delinquency* and juvenile *delinquents* have common referents, but they are not the same thing. Neither is homogeneous with respect to either the law or those who break them, and neither is static, either as an idea or as behavior. They have changed over the years, and they continue to change.

- Study of the past informs both the present and likely or possible futures.
- Juvenile courts, which have responsibility for administration of laws concerning juvenile delinquency and juvenile delinquents, also receive cases of child abuse and neglect, and other living conditions of children.
- Juvenile courts vary a great deal in different jurisdictions (states, counties, and cities), and these, too, continue to change in response to changing social conditions.
- Juvenile delinquency concerns *children and childhood*, both of which have changed greatly over time and continue to change.
- Juvenile delinquency and the children who are called delinquents are *social problems*. Social problems require *civic engagement*, which also has changed over the years. As citizens, you—our readers—are in part responsible for the manner in which society responds to these problems today and, more importantly, in the future. It is important, therefore, that you understand how and why civic engagement occurs in order to participate in bringing about change, today and in the future.

History offers no panaceas for the present, but it does help to alert us to the temptation of self-deception in dealing with a problem no more soluble today than it was a century and a half ago.

(Steven L. Schlossman, 1977, p. 193)

Note that a common thread running through each of these points is a focus on *social change*, which throughout this book will be an important lens through which we will study juvenile delinquency and juvenile delinquents. Understanding how social change affects our subject matter requires historical perspective. In addition, methods developed by the social sciences will provide the principal means by which we will try to understand delinquency and delinquents and what might be done about them. Although neither science nor history can tell us what *should* be done about any social problem, both are important tools for understanding and for social policy concerning all social problems.

Life is both a product and a creator of history, just as history informs life, as in the quotation at the beginning of this chapter. Thus, history is an important *context* for understanding juvenile delinquency—one of many contexts that we will examine in this book.

> *Context: (kon'tekst), noun* 1. *the parts of a written or spoken statement that precede or follow a specific word. You have misinterpreted my sentence because you took it out of context.* 2. *the set of circumstances or facts that surround a particular event, situation, etc.*
> (Webster's Encyclopedic Dictionary of the English Language)
>
> *Contextualize: Place in or treat as part of a context; study in context.*
> (Oxford English Dictionary)

Just as the circumstances (*contexts*) in which we use words are important to our intended meaning, and the circumstances surrounding events and situations are important to how we understand them, we cannot understand juvenile delinquency without knowing the *contexts* in which it occurs. In this chapter, we examine the *historical* contexts that resulted in the "discovery" of childhood, which in turn preceded the "invention" of the *juvenile court*.

We do not ordinarily think of childhood, a commonly understood stage of life, as requiring discovery, or of institutions such as courts as being invented. History tells us, however, that childhood has not always been recognized as a stage of life requiring special treatment, and laws defining juvenile delinquency and courts dedicated to them did not always exist. Historical contexts of ideas and practices toward children and those that were associated with the creation of laws and courts are especially important, for without them neither juvenile delinquency nor juvenile delinquents would exist.

Why *delinquency* and *delinquents*? The distinction between these terms is important and, for the most part, straightforward. Juvenile *delinquency* refers to the *behavior* that is described in legal statutes as such. Juvenile *delinquents* are children who behave in ways that those statutes define as delinquent. As noted above, however, the statutes also define certain *living conditions* of children as falling within the jurisdiction of juvenile courts. Moreover, not all children who live in these conditions, or who behave in ways defined as delinquent, come to the attention of juvenile courts. How they come to the attention of the courts is an important part of understanding the nature of juvenile delinquency.

Laws and their enforcement have consequences not only for children but also for their parents, for police and other authorities, and for communities. Families, communities, laws, and courts are also important contexts in which delinquent behavior occurs and is responded to. And they are among the most important places and institutional contexts for understanding why children behave as they do, and how and why such behavior occurs in such contexts. So also, as we shall see, are schools, street corners and parks, and other public and private places.

Juvenile delinquency is not confined to *local* contexts, however. Increasingly, the impacts of events occurring in far off places are felt in local communities. No matter where we live, global political, economic, and broader social forces influence our lives. But we are getting ahead of our story. We will return to the effects of global forces in the final chapter of the book. First we must consider what we mean when we refer to the "discovery" of childhood.

CHILDHOOD: FROM DISCOVERY TO PREOCCUPATION

"Childhood" is an idea as well as a stage of life. There have always been children, of course, but only in recent centuries has childhood been recognized as having special status. The French historian of family life Philippe Aries concluded that

> In the Middle Ages, at the beginning of modern times, and for a long time after that in the lower classes, children were mixed with adults as soon as they were considered capable of doing without their mothers or nannies, not long after a tardy weaning (in other words, at about the age of seven). (Aries, 1962, p. 411)

Aries based his analysis on paintings, diaries, and writings over a period of four centuries. Prior to the twelfth century, he noted, children were portrayed in art simply as *little adults* (Aries, 1962).[1] Even the baby Jesus was pictured as "an adult on a reduced scale" (p. 35).

The *family* was also regarded quite differently in earlier times. It fulfilled certain functions: "it ensured the transmission of life, property and names; but it did not penetrate very far into human sensibility." Most importantly for present purposes, "it had no idea of education" (Aries, 1962, p. 411).

No aspect of childhood has changed more over the centuries than the *treatment* of children. Lloyd DeMause's introduction of his book *The History of Childhood* is graphic and dramatic:

> The history of childhood is a nightmare from which mankind has only recently begun to awaken. The further back in history one digs, the more archaic the mode of parenting, and the more likely children are to be routinely abandoned, killed, beaten, emotionally and physically starved, and sexually molested. (DeMause, 1973, p. 1)

During this "early modern" period, the prevailing view of babies and very young children was one largely of *indifference*. Historians disagree on details concerning the extent to which indifference was accompanied by brutality, but they agree that harsh material conditions and high infant mortality played a large role in how children were viewed and the ways they were treated. With lack of medical knowledge and with primitive technologies of communication and transportation (which today make possible quick and effective response to diseases, accidents, and assaults), the life of children as recently as a century ago was precarious at best.[2] Survival beyond the teen years was problematic. Under such conditions, it was unwise to become closely attached to children who might not survive.

Lack of knowledge and harsh living conditions were not the only influences on child care, however. Beliefs and attitudes were also involved, and these, too, changed greatly over time. We begin with consideration of beliefs and attitudes among Europeans following the collapse of Greco-Roman civilization.[3]

Historian John Sommerville notes that the "period between the fall of Rome and the year 1000 is the most obscure in all of Western history" (Sommerville, 1990, p. 66). We know that "(c)ivilization remained in a perilous state for centuries. . . . Very likely there was no one who could afford the luxury of enjoying or encouraging children simply for their own sake" (p. 69).[4]

Concern for the welfare of children survived the depredations of the barbarians as even they settled down and Western civilization reasserted itself. Two sixteenth-century historical changes were especially important for child rearing: (1) changes and conflicts among religious institutions; and (2) the ascendancy of the nation state.

Disagreements about how children should be reared were common features of the sometimes-bitter controversies and conflicts between the Catholic Church and emerging Protestant doctrines and churches (who also contested among themselves) during the sixteenth century. Having thus been "discovered," childhood became a major preoccupation and a source of great controversy.[5] Despite their differences in doctrine and practice, however, Catholics and Protestants alike agreed that *early* child training was important.

As these changes were occurring among religions, the *governance* of European societies was also changing. The ability of powerful aristocratic families to govern weakened as central governments consolidated power. At the same time, the participation in governance of citizens (mostly men early on and for a long time after) expanded greatly.

Relationships between religious and governmental authorities, and of both with families, have always been complex and often conflicted. Children sometimes became pawns in such conflicts. Sommerville's conclusion to a chapter he calls "The Nation-State Takes up Child Care" is instructive:

> Because the growing power of the state had helped to weaken the family, the state had tried to take up some of the

responsibility families could no longer carry. The net effect, though, may have been to weaken the sense of family responsibility still further. As the state reached the end of its resources, the wealthier classes demonstrated their goodwill toward children by philanthropy. But even this sentimental indulgence may have had a negative effect if it blinded society to the growing abuses of that century. By the late eighteenth century parish children were being sent into the growing navy as "powder monkeys" and into the new factories, where they were worked until they dropped. For as Britain and the other states of Europe began their imperial and industrial competition, children were being given increasingly grim roles at the bottom of society. By ignoring such conditions, these nations had actually encouraged the abuses which they later tried to curb. (Sommerville, 1990, p. 123)

Child-rearing practices and concerns continued to evolve as societies sought to correct such abuses. Some of the most important changes had their roots in what was to become the new nation of the United States of America (USA).

A NEW NATION "GROWS UP": THE USA

The documentary record of the *behavior* of children in colonial America is scant, but it is clear that views of children and their control reflected local social conditions and beliefs in each colony. Two examples are illustrative.

A strict puritanical code governed the Massachusetts Bay Colony. Crime and sin were considered interchangeable, and many behaviors of either type were punishable by death. Age was considered a mitigating factor, however, as shown in the following excerpt from Edwin Powers' discussion of capital crimes in the laws of the colony:

> ... for sodomy ... children under fourteen were to be "severely punished" but not executed; for cursing and smiting parents ... only those "above sixteen years old, and of sufficient understanding" could be put to death; for being stubborn or rebellious sons ... only those "of sufficient years and understanding (*viz.*) sixteen years of age" were liable; for arson, the law also applies only to those "of the age of sixteen years and upward"; for "denying the Scriptures to the infallible word of God," again the minimum age was sixteen for those who were liable to the death penalty. (Powers, 1966, reprinted in Lerman, 1970, p. 8)

Despite these harsh provisions, Powers concludes that "the courts exhibited a surprising degree of humane and kindly treatment toward the very young, usually referring the willful, unruly, or disobedient child to his parents for correction. Young children were not publicly whipped, and ... probably no child under fifteen was executed" (p. 10).

The need for laborers in the colonies led to abuses, however, as when agents were contracted with for supplying apprentices and indentured servants. Bremner's study of *Children and Youth in America* (1970) notes that children from the streets and asylums of England were often "recruited" by questionable means for such service. A 1619 document addressed to the city of London from the Virginia Company explains the system, first expressing gratitude for supplying "one hundred children this last year, which by the goodness of God there safely arrived (save such as died in the way)." The chief purpose of the document, however, is revealed in the next paragraph:

> ... we pray your Lordship and the rest in pursuit of your former so pious actions to renew your like favors and furnish us again with one hundred more for the next spring. Our desire is that we may have them of twelve years old and upward.... they shall be apprentices, the boys until they come to twenty-one years of age, the girls till the like age or till they be married, and afterwards they shall be placed as tenants upon the public land with best conditions where they shall have houses with stock of corn and cattle to begin with, and afterward the moiety of all increase and profit whatsoever. (Bremner, 1970, vol. 1, p. 7)

> *Our nation was conceived and born in violence...*
> *(Richard Maxwell Brown, 1979, p. 20)*

Despite such abuses, early colonial American settlements were characterized by a close sense of community and by effective social control. By the time of the revolutionary war, however, this sense had deteriorated, particularly in larger cities. Opposition to colonial authorities, symbolized by the slogan "taxation without representation," grew along with increased sentiment for independence from England. Historian Richard Wade concludes that in the run-up to the revolution "rioting and organized physical force was part of the politics of the colonies" (Wade, 1969, p. 353). As the Richard Maxwell Brown quotation (above) notes, "Such was the Boston Massacre of 1770, in which five defiant Americans were killed by British officers and troops who were goaded by patriotic roughnecks. The whole episode was a natural continuation of nearly a century of organized mob violence in Boston"

(Brown, 1979, p. 20). Women and children—even clergy—participated in protest and rioting in Philadelphia, and juvenile misbehavior "was endemic" (Geffen, 1978, p. 113).

Social change accelerated following the revolutionary war. The country became more industrialized and the population grew rapidly as immigrants flooded into the cities and the frontier continued to expand. Social control became even more problematic as other problems multiplied: racial and ethnic conflict, public health, child labor, and increasing poverty and crime. Many young people were caught up in riots that plagued large cities, such as New York, Boston, and Philadelphia. As governments and other institutions struggled to cope with change and instability, fear of crime and immorality fueled concern for the upbringing of children, stimulating calls for reform.

When it came, reform took many forms, perhaps none more important for what was to become the juvenile court system than the establishment of metropolitan police forces, the first example of which occurred in London at the behest of Sir Robert Peel (hence, the English "Bobbies"). Prior to the establishment of municipal police, citizens had little recourse when they were victimized by crime, which by several accounts was rampant in eighteenth- and early nineteenth-century London.[6] Although the need to respond to increasing mob violence in large cities was the original impetus for creating municipal police in this country, crime control and public order rapidly became the major goals. Most importantly, the police soon came to be the most common resource for citizens who experienced minor crimes, public nuisances, and rowdiness—just the sort of behaviors that comprise such an important part of juvenile delinquency. As Lane remarks, "while private individuals may make the effort to initiate the processes of justice when directly injured, professionals are required to deal, in number, with those whose merely immoral or distasteful behavior hurts no one in particular" (Lane, 1969, p. 362). The police, as we shall see, became a critical element in the juvenile justice system.

Even before the first metropolitan police were established in this country, a widespread social movement had begun to create "penitentiaries for the criminal, asylums for the insane, almshouses for the poor, orphan asylums for homeless children" (Rothman, 1971, p. xii). Among these was the New York House of Refuge established in 1824, the first of its kind in the United States. An early report from this institution spelled out its rationale (from Lerman, 1970, pp. 13–14):

> In New York, as in every large city, there were a number of forsaken children, many of them orphans, and many who derived no protection from parents, who received no instruction from them but in wickedness and profanity, and no example but in the practice of vice and immorality. These destitute beings began life by resorting to dishonest means to maintain it and became criminal in their infancy. . . . When the same walls enclosed old and young offenders, the consequences were such as must have been expected. From the moment a child was obnoxious to a criminal proceeding, he was lost. There could be no hope of saving him from destruction, if he were innocent, or of reforming him if he were guilty. . . . The (New York) legislature has very much enlarged the objects of our institution, and entrusted to its managers powers that have not heretofore been delegated. . . . If a child be found destitute—if abandoned by its parents—or suffered to lead a vicious or vagrant life; or if convicted of any crime, it may be sent to the House of Refuge. There is in no case any other sentence than that it shall "there be dealt with according to law." That is, it may if not released by some legal process, be there

course, are not perfect. They sometimes err by neglect or abuse, or even by example, and so it was with super-parent juvenile courts. The power of the state, through the court, to preempt parental authority without safeguards for the rights of children and parents was under attack even before the first juvenile court was established in 1899.[9] How this has played out is the subject of the next chapter. But first we need to outline our hopes for the remainder of the book.

Chapter 2 discusses the continuing evolution of the juvenile court and changes in police organization and practices, that is, how they have adapted to changes in the larger society and the consequences of those changes. Next, in Chapter 3, we discuss the ways in which social scientists and others study juvenile delinquency and juvenile delinquents.

Chapter 4 presents data from various sources describing the social distribution of delinquency and delinquents, that is, where they are located within communities. The following chapter (Chapter 5) discusses theories that attempt to explain the social distribution of delinquency and why delinquents behave as they do. The data presented in Chapter 4 do not "speak for themselves." They have been interpreted in a variety of ways as social scientists and others have tried to understand and explain them. Here we will discuss other types of evidence about delinquency and delinquents and various *theoretical perspectives* about how and why they occur as they do.

The last two chapters build on what has gone before. We turn first, in Chapter 6, to efforts to control delinquency, including programs designed to prevent its occurrence and to treat delinquent individuals and groups. The book closes, in Chapter 7, by considering global economic, political, and social forces that affect us all, and some of the implications of these forces for young people, their role in societies throughout the world, and their behavior.

NOTES

1. Greek art was an exception. Following the Roman conquest, however, children were again portrayed as little men and women.

2. When she was 89 years old, Jim Short's mother recalled that, at the age of 9 (in the year 1909), she was once taken in a horse-drawn ambulance to a city hospital 15 miles from her farm residence.

3. For a brief review of family and state concerns with children in ancient Greece and Rome, see the work of Sommerville (1990). Most of what we know about the history of childhood in Western societies is based on accounts of European child-rearing beliefs and practices. We do not here review accounts of child rearing in primitive or non-Western societies.

4. "The one major institution that did survive Rome's fall was the Church" (Sommerville, 1990, p. 63). The Church not only survived, but may have "saved civilization," by Cahill's lucid and entertaining account. See his *How the Irish Saved Civilization* (1995).

5. Sommerville (1990, p. 103) suggests that early Protestants may have been "the first group that doubted that beating would save their children" from eternal damnation.

6. See Allen Silver's (1967) excellent essay on "The demand for order in civil society."

7. Correctional work at this time was closely associated with the medical, as well as legal, professions. Crime and delinquency were thus viewed as "curable" much like disease.

8. The ancient doctrine of *parens patriae*, in feudal England, gave broad authority over the welfare of children to the King, as the symbolic father of all his subjects.

9. Laws that established juvenile courts were enacted at the state level. Only in 1974, with passage of the Juvenile Justice and Prevention Act, did the federal government recognize that there might be such a federal responsibility.

2 | THE CONTINUING EVOLUTION OF THE JUVENILE COURT SYSTEM AND ITS CONSEQUENCES

Change did not stop in the aftermath of the tidal wave of changes following establishment of the first juvenile court. As juvenile courts evolved, the detached and formal model of justice found in adult criminal courts eventually was replaced by a "hands on" and more nurturing approach. New laws were written, decisions were made on the basis of the child's best interest, and professionals and caring adults were encouraged to get involved and be part of the process. As a sign of the times, the new terminology marking the contrast substituted euphemisms such as "detain," "refer to court," "adjudicate," "disposition," and "training school" for criminal courts' "arrest," "charge," "convict," "sentence," and "prison" (Clear, Cole, & Reisig, 2006, p. 433).

Cracks soon appeared in the developing system. The ambiguity of statutes defining behaviors that could bring young people under the jurisdiction of juvenile courts led to abuses of children and violations of their civil rights and those of their parents. Frequent legal challenges led eventually to review by the U.S. Supreme Court. In the process, the philosophy and the procedures of juvenile courts were altered. Social change and new social problems also posed new challenges, and the shifting political climate proved divisive. From the very beginning, the mission of juvenile courts and relationships with the criminal court system had been called into question. Change was inevitable.

Courts were not the only changing aspect of American justice. Police departments, facing conflicting demands and heavy pressures to reform, sought to rationalize and legitimize their occupation by adopting higher educational standards, certification requirements, and technical improvements in command, communications, and crime detection. Although these marks of professionalization fostered greater accountability and helped to check abuses of police discretion, they also promoted a detached outlook that ultimately contributed to more severe handling of juveniles, as shown in Table 2.1. More cases were brought before juvenile courts, and fewer were referred to other agencies or handled within the department and released.

The rapid influx of cases continued through the present "get tough" era, exacerbating emerging problems in the juvenile court system, including ambiguities in both mission and reach. Early juvenile court laws had been the sole province of individual states, and there was much variation in such matters as the age of court jurisdiction and behaviors for which children might be brought before the court. Statutes defining juvenile delinquency, dependency, and child neglect were in fact extremely vague and often contradictory. A list of "personality traits and types of behavior" for the purpose of identifying and treating potential delinquents included both "overactivity" and "underactivity," for example, "bashfulness" as well as "show-off behavior," "finicalness" and "lack of orderliness," as well as "dependence," "defiance," and "silliness" (Hakeem, 1957–58). Given such uncertainty, it is hardly surprising that the laws were subject to abuse, and were for critics a further indication of the failure of the juvenile court system.

TABLE 2.1 POLICE DISPOSITION OF JUVENILES TAKEN INTO CUSTODY, 1990–2005, BY SIZE OF PLACE

Disposition	Year	All Agencies Reporting (%)	All Cities Reporting (%)	Large Cities 250,000+ (%)	Cities 100,000 to 249,999 (%)	Cities 50,000 to 99,999 (%)	Cities 25,000 to 49,999 (%)	Cities 10,000 to 24,999 (%)	Under 10,000 (%)	Suburban[a] Area (%)	Rural[b] (%)
Handled within department and released	1961		45.3	36.2	44.4	50.1	53.9	54.4	51.5	(No report)	43.4[c]
	1965		47.1	38.5	48.9	54.6	51.5	52.5	50.4	56.3	29.6
	1970		45.7	37.7	43.6	50.2	48.6	51.0	48.7	52.6	33.4
	1975		42.8	29.5	44.3	49.1	46.2	47.8	43.7	49.6	29.8
	1980		34.5	26.0	35.8	35.9	37.8	38.0	34.8	38.8	27.4
	1985		31.4	25.7	30.8	35.1	34.1	34.8	30.5	29.3	20.8
	1990	28.3	29.4	25.3	31.0	33.4	31.1	29.2	26.8	32.5	21.1
	1995	28.4	27.4	25.8	27.2	29.7	28.6	27.1	27.1	33.0	35.8
	2000	20.3	21.0	27.6	17.2	19.8	19.3	18.4	18.9	20.0	16.1
	2005	20.2	21.1	31.5	18.6	20.3	17.6	16.2	15.9	17.8	15.8
Referred to juvenile court	1961		48.9	59.8	52.7	40.7	39.0	38.9	38.8	(No report)	47.3
	1965		45.8	53.6	44.8	39.2	42.0	40.6	42.3	37.6	56.4

(*continued*)

Disposition	Year	All Agencies Reporting (%)	All Cities Reporting (%)	Large Cities 250,000+ (%)	Cities 100,000 to 249,999 (%)	Cities 50,000 to 99,999 (%)	Cities 25,000 to 49,999 (%)	Cities 10,000 to 24,999 (%)	Under 10,000 (%)	Suburban[a] Area (%)	Rural[b] (%)
	1970		49.8	58.9	52.7	45.4	45.4	44.2	45.9	42.0	58.1
	1975		51.7	67.0	51.4	45.1	47.8	46.2	48.2	45.1	61.7
	1980		57.2	69.2	57.7	55.4	54.4	52.8	51.9	52.6	61.8
	1985		60.9	71.0	64.2	56.1	56.9	56.0	56.4	65.6	67.8
	1990	64.5	63.7	72.5	64.4	57.8	62.6	62.1	61.5	59.1	66.6
	1995	65.7	66.8	69.1	65.2	65.9	65.4	67.1	66.4	61.4	58.3
	2000	70.8	70.4	66.6	77.0	73.4	72.5	69.2	67.3	69.6	70.8
	2005	70.7	70.3	67.6	73.7	71.3	72.4	70.0	68.8	69.9	68.2
Referred to welfare agency	1961		2.0	1.8	1.3	2.8	2.6	1.7	1.7	(No report)	1.6[c]
	1965		3.1	6.1	1.4	2.1	1.2	1.2	1.3	1.0	2.0
	1970		1.6	2.2	1.6	1.4	1.8	0.8	0.9	1.2	2.2
	1975		1.4	1.6	1.5	1.5	1.2	1.2	1.3	1.1	2.0
	1980		1.5	1.1	2.6	2.3	1.2	1.2	1.1	1.2	2.3
	1985		1.9	1.6	2.9	2.1	2.4	1.4	1.4	1.7	2.2

(continued)

Disposition	Year	All Agencies Reporting (%)	All Cities Reporting (%)	Large Cities 250,000+ (%)	Cities 100,000 to 249,999 (%)	Cities 50,000 to 99,999 (%)	Cities 25,000 to 49,999 (%)	Cities 10,000 to 24,999 (%)	Under 10,000 (%)	Suburban[a] Area (%)	Rural[b] (%)
Referred to other police agency	1990	1.6	1.5	0.7	1.8	2.1	1.4	1.7	1.6	1.5	3.6
	1995	1.7	1.7	1.9	2.6	1.9	1.2	1.2	1.2	1.2	1.3
	2000	0.8	0.8	1.4	0.8	0.6	1.2	0.5	0.4	0.6	1.1
	2005	0.4	0.3	0.1	0.2	0.6	0.4	0.4	0.4	0.5	0.8
	1961		2.9	2.0	1.2	5.6	3.0	3.6	4.2	(No report)	3.9[c]
	1965		2.7	1.5	3.0	3.3	3.5	3.4	3.2	3.6	3.7
	1970		2.1	1.0	1.7	2.4	3.0	2.7	2.7	3.2	4.3
	1975		1.8	1.1	1.3	2.5	1.9	1.9	2.3	2.0	2.8
	1980		1.7	2.4	2.0	1.6	1.8	1.3	1.4	1.5	2.6
	1985		1.1	1.2	0.7	1.4	1.1	1.1	1.3	0.9	2.5
	1990	1.1	1.1	0.9	0.7	1.4	1.2	1.2	0.9	1.2	1.7
	1995	0.9	0.8	0.8	0.8	0.4	1.2	0.9	0.7	1.1	1.6
	2000	1.1	1.1	0.4	1.0	1.0	2.3	1.4	1.0	0.9	0.9
	2005	1.3	1.1	0.3	2.7	1.4	1.7	0.5	0.8	1.3	1.2

(continued)

Disposition	Year	All Agencies Reporting (%)	All Cities Reporting (%)	Large Cities 250,000+ (%)	Cities 100,000 to 249,999 (%)	Cities 50,000 to 99,999 (%)	Cities 25,000 to 49,999 (%)	Cities 10,000 to 24,999 (%)	Under 10,000 (%)	Suburban[a] Area (%)	Rural[b] (%)
Referred to criminal or adult court	1961		0.9	0.1	0.4	0.7	1.5	1.3	3.8	(No report)	3.8[c]
	1965		1.4	0.4	1.9	0.7	1.7	2.3	3.7	1.5	8.3
	1970		0.8	0.2	0.5	0.6	1.3	1.3	1.7	1.0	2.0
	1975		2.3	0.9	1.5	1.8	3.0	2.9	4.5	2.2	3.6
	1980		5.1	1.3	1.8	4.8	4.6	6.7	10.8	6.1	5.9
	1985		4.6	0.5	1.3	5.3	5.4	6.7	10.3	2.5	6.7
	1990	4.5	4.3	0.6	2.1	5.4	3.8	5.9	9.2	5.8	6.9
	1995	3.3	3.3	2.4	4.3	2.0	3.6	3.8	4.6	3.3	3.0
	2000	7.0	6.7	4.0	4.0	5.2	4.7	10.5	12.3	9.0	11.1
	2005	7.4	7.0	0.5	4.8	6.3	7.9	12.9	14.1	10.5	14.0

[a] Includes areas in other city groups.

[b] Rural counties reported in 1995 and 2000; nonmetropolitan county reported in 2005.

[c] "County agencies" reported in 1961; rural agencies from 1965 to 1990.

Source: Federal Bureau of Investigation (1961, 1965, 1970, 1975, 1980, 1990, 1995, 2000, 2005).

CHALLENGES TO THE JUVENILE COURT SYSTEM

Court challenges and social changes in post-WWII America had repercussions in both criminal and juvenile justice systems. The bifurcation of the two systems eroded in response to sometimes contradictory concerns: (1) the civil rights movement, including the rights of juveniles under the law; (2) fears that indulgent child-rearing practices were contributing to rising crime rates, especially among young minority (chiefly black) males; and (3) moral concerns associated with musical styles, drug use, and "hippie" life styles, coupled with political activism of baby-boomer's children in opposition to the Vietnam War and in support of civil rights. Paradoxically, the resulting societal backlash coincided with pressures from the legal profession and social scientists to avoid stigmatizing young delinquents and criminals with official records and incarceration, as evidenced in the conclusion of the 1960s crime commission:

> . . . the experience of more than half a century has made clear that, despite the hopes and best efforts of those involved in the juvenile courts, being adjudicated delinquent has become as stigmatizing as being convicted as a criminal. In the minds of the child, the family, and the community, including schools, the Government, the Armed Forces, and future employers, the label of juvenile delinquent imposes a severe and grievous disadvantage upon the child. (President's Commission on Law Enforcement and Administration of Justice, 1967, p. 30)

Despite the determination of the early child savers to separate juveniles from criminal courts, distinctions between the two systems continued to erode. Although case work theory, based on careful attention to individual children and their circumstances, had come to dominate court ideology, the reality was quite different. As more and more children were brought under coercive control, some children were seriously mistreated and the reach of the courts into private family matters offended many. Juvenile courts were failing in their most basic mission: protecting the welfare of children.

THE UNITED STATES SUPREME COURT

The mid-1960s marked the beginning of what was to become the heyday of legal challenges to juvenile court legislation and practice. Although focused more on due process than on juvenile court philosophy, the rulings of the U.S. Supreme Court led to a massive overhauling of the system.

The first landmark ruling was pronounced in *Kent v. United States* (1966), a case centered on the procedures by which juveniles could be transferred to criminal court. Morris Kent was 16 years old when he was arrested and charged with rape, burglary, and robbery in the District of Columbia. Denied access to an attorney and unaware of his legal right to remain silent, Kent succumbed to the pressures of extensive police interrogation and confessed to each of the alleged crimes. On his own authority and without clear justification, the presiding juvenile judge transferred young Kent to criminal court jurisdiction, where he was eventually tried by a jury and found guilty. On appeal by Kent's lawyer, the U.S. Supreme Court overturned the conviction, ruling that Kent had been denied access to an attorney, a court hearing prior to transfer, and other "essentials of due process" to which juveniles are entitled.

Kent was followed a year later by a much broader ruling, *In re Gault*. Gerald Gault had been found delinquent by an Arizona juvenile court for making obscene phone calls to his neighbor, Mrs. Cook. His sentence—commitment to the State Industrial School until age 21—was far more severe than the maximum of two months' imprisonment he would have received *had he been an adult*. After the Arizona Supreme Court refused to overturn the Superior Court's dismissal of the writ of habeas corpus filed by Gault's attorney, appeal was made to the U.S. Supreme Court.

The issue before the court once again concerned the right of juveniles to due process. With the *Kent* ruling, some of the Supreme Court justices expressed grave concern that juvenile courts had become a virtual no man's land, where children received "neither the protections accorded to adults nor the solicitous care and regenerative treatment postulated for children" (Justice Fortas, quoted in Stapleton & Teitelbaum, 1972, p. 28). The Court's decision in *Gault*, parts of which are presented here, reflected this thinking and brought about new ways of shielding children from the awesome power of the state:

1. Notice, to comply with due process requirements, must be given sufficiently in advance of scheduled court proceedings so that reasonable opportunity to prepare will be afforded, and it must "set forth the alleged misconduct with particularity."
2. A proceeding where the issue is whether the child will be found to be "delinquent" and subjected to the loss of his liberty for years is comparable in seriousness to a felony prosecution. The juvenile needs the assistance of counsel to cope with problems of law, to make skilled inquiry into the facts, to insist upon regularity of the proceedings, and to ascertain whether he has a defense and to prepare and submit it. The child "requires the guiding hand of counsel at every step in the proceedings against him."
3. . . . absent a valid confession, a determination of delinquency and an order of commitment to a state institution cannot be sustained

in the absence of sworn testimony subject to the opportunity for cross-examination in accordance with our law and constitutional requirements.

4. We conclude that the constitutional privilege against self-incrimination is applicable in the case of juveniles as it is with respect to adults. We appreciate that special problems may arise with respect to waiver of the privilege by or on behalf of children, and that there may well be some differences in technique—but not in principle—depending upon the age of the child and the presence and competence of parents. The participation of counsel will, of course, assist the police, juvenile courts and appellate tribunals in administering the privilege. If counsel is not present for some permissible reason when an admission is obtained, the greatest care must be taken to assure that the admission was voluntary, in the sense not only that it has not been coerced or suggested, but also that it is not the product of ignorance of rights or of adolescent fantasy, fright or despair.[1]

Justice Stewart's dissenting opinion argued that preoccupation with traditional legal concerns threatened to undermine the "enlightened" ideals upon which the juvenile court was founded. Heeding this warning, the Court ruled in *McKeiver v. Pennsylvania* (1971) that providing juveniles with an automatic right to a jury trial would transform juvenile courts into an adversarial, adult-like system and depart too drastically from the philosophy of *parens patriae* and related notions of rehabilitation. In other rulings, however, the Court abandoned this logic and sided with those who wished to see juveniles granted the same due process protections guaranteed to adults in criminal courts. For example, juvenile hearings, particularly those concerning the possibility of a substantial loss of freedom, were ruled as the legal equivalent of criminal proceedings and could no longer be treated as civil matters. Persons adjudicated in juvenile court were to be protected under the double jeopardy clause of the Fifth Amendment from subsequent conviction in criminal courts (*Breed v. Jones*, 1975), and the relevant standard of guilt would be "proof beyond a reasonable doubt," rather than the lesser requirement of a "preponderance of evidence" as in civil cases (*In re Winship*, 1970).

THE FEDERAL GOVERNMENT

Only after the first Supreme Court decisions requiring legal safeguards for the rights of children did the legislative and executive branches of the federal government begin to play a more active role in juvenile justice. Broader social changes and a more reform-minded federal government were also in play. By the mid-1960s, the country had been ripped apart by the tragic assassinations of John F. Kennedy and other political leaders; tensions related to poverty, racial and other inequalities, and clashes over civil rights and the Vietnam War were widespread, and the nuclear arms race was in full swing. Even more than his predecessor, President Lyndon Johnson responded to the social problems of the day with a massive expansion of the American welfare state, emphasizing economic progress and declaring in his State of the Union address an all out "war on poverty." Within just two years of this famous speech, an unprecedented amount of antipoverty legislation had been enacted.

> The Economic Opportunity Act (1964) provided the basis for the Office of Economic Opportunity (OEO), the Job Corps, Volunteers in Service to America (VISTA), Upward Bound, Head Start, Legal Services, the Neighborhood Youth Corps, the Community Action Program (CAP), the college Work-Study program, Neighborhood Development Centers, small business loan programs, rural programs, migrant worker programs,

remedial education projects, local health care centers, and others. The antipoverty effort, however, did not stop there. It encompassed a range of Great Society legislation far broader than the Economic Opportunity Act alone. Other important measures with antipoverty functions included an $11 billion tax cut (Revenue Act of 1964), the Civil Rights Act (1964), the Food Stamp Act (1964), the Elementary and Secondary Education Act (1965), the Higher Education Act (1965), the Social Security amendments creating Medicare/Medicaid (1965), the creation of the Department of Housing and Urban Development (1965), the Voting Rights Act (1965), the Model Cities Act (1966), the Fair Housing Act (1968), several job-training programs, and various Urban Renewal-related projects. (Germany, 2007, p. 1)

Drawing inspiration from the Chicago school of urban sociology, the President's Committee on Juvenile Delinquency and Youth Crime adopted *community action* as a cornerstone of public policy. The war on Poverty built on this ideal, to the delight of some and the dismay of others. Critics charged that there was both wasteful spending and corruption and that a culture of dependency had been created among the lower classes. In the end, poverty outlasted both antipoverty campaigns and a backlash centered on individual responsibility and resulting in massive cutbacks of community programs and investments. Although many social ills remained intransigent, the effects of federal activism were by then complex and far-reaching, extending to virtually every facet of society.

WHAT TO DO WITH STATUS OFFENDERS?

Because behaviors such as disobeying parents, consumption of alcohol, and truancy would not be subject to court intervention if committed by adults, children who are brought before the court for such "offenses" are referred to as "status offenders" (Maxson & Klein, 1997, p. 4). Throughout much of the early history of the juvenile justice system, imprisonment of status offenders and other types of formal intervention were justified on the grounds that such behaviors were precursors to more serious crimes. In 1967, through its *Task Force Report on Juvenile Delinquency*, the President's Commission on Law Enforcement and the Administration of Justice recommended that status offenders be separated from delinquents and kept out of institutions of confinement.

Others agreed, and enactment of the Juvenile Justice and Delinquency Prevention Act (JJDPA) in 1974 mandated that states begin the process of removing status offenders from detention and correctional facilities. Careful research by Cheryl Maxson and Malcolm Klein, however, demonstrated that deinstitutionalization of status offenders was more difficult than had been anticipated:

> ... many officials and practitioners, to say nothing of the general public, were reluctant to turn loose troublesome kids for the very reason that they were troublesome. They were thought to need treatment, or control, or both. ... Programs to treat and/or control had to be put in place as alternatives to confinement. Suitable community mechanisms had to be identified or developed that were capable of dealing with habitual truants, kids defiant of their parents, alcohol users, precocious sex offenders, and—most challenging of all—repeat runaways. (Maxson & Klein, 1997, p. 7)

Given these challenges, it is no surprise that the first national assessment of progress toward deinstitutionalizing status offenders (DSO I) yielded disappointing results. In addition to bringing to light glaring inconsistencies in practices across states, "project data on many thousands of youth failed to demonstrate the advantages of community treatment and in fact seemed to point to its deleterious effects on many of the youth involved" (Maxson & Klein, 1997, p. 189). Such findings did not sit well with the Office of Juvenile Justice and Delinquency Prevention (OJJDP),[2] and so were downplayed rather than used in the development of sound policy.

By the mid-1980s, political winds had shifted and there was little official tolerance for the deinstitutionalization of status offenders. Hoping to confirm the superiority of a model emphasizing deterrence and individual accountability, OJJDP again solicited and funded an evaluation of the effects of deinstitutionalizing status offenders. Contrary to expectations, the study showed that the practices of social agencies were largely unrelated to legislative philosophy and intent, whether treatment-oriented or centered on deterrence principles. And again, OJJDP refused to publish the study, findings from which eventually appeared in *Responding to Troubled Youth* (Maxson & Klein, 1997).

Since 1997, the number of status offenders committed and held in residential facilities has decreased considerably. Except in a few states, status offenses comprise only a small proportion of the caseload of juvenile courts. Nonetheless, states continue to grapple with the question of what to do with status offenders, so many of whom are young girls fleeing traumatic home environments. In 2003, nearly 5,000 status offenders were included in the 96,655 juveniles in residential placement. In contrast to juveniles adjudged as delinquents, more than 2/3 of status offenders were housed in private facilities. The median *time served* by status offenders was 105 days, only 3 weeks shorter than the average for aggravated assault offenders and nearly identical to the average for juveniles committed for weapons offenses, auto theft, burglary, or theft.

LAW AND ORDER

The change toward a "get tough" crime control model brought about new aims, practices, and challenges. Largely in response to public outcry and fears concerning rising crime rates (including a purported new wave of hyper-violent teens), particularly in urban and minority communities, the juvenile court system was transformed "from a nominally rehabilitative social welfare agency into a scaled-down second-class criminal court for young people" (Feld, 1999, p. 3). Juvenile court reforms of the past were regarded as far too lenient and insensitive to the rights of victims. Why permit young killers and rapists to remain in the community on probation or spend a few years in a juvenile facility, only to be set free once they reach the age of adulthood?

In this context, past court reforms and protections were challenged in many ways. Being "tough on crime," whether committed by adults or juveniles, became politically attractive, even necessary. Many states revised the *purpose* clauses of juvenile codes to reflect renewed emphasis on individual accountability, punishment, and risk containment. OJJDP began a program of Juvenile Accountability Block Grants to states. The adoption of state sentencing guidelines by the federal government and nearly 20 states effectively reduced the discretionary authority of judges and transferred decision-making power into the hands of state and federal prosecutors and legislatures. States increased use of waivers to adult court, in some cases enacting statutory exclusion provisions that bypassed juvenile courts altogether. In general, such laws lowered the age at which juveniles could be transferred to criminal courts, expanded the number of crimes for transfer, and changed transfer processes.

Although little research has been devoted to the effects of these changes, studies suggest that youth who are transferred to criminal courts are more likely to recidivate than those handled in juvenile courts. In one state, Texas, juveniles who were transferred to criminal court spent less

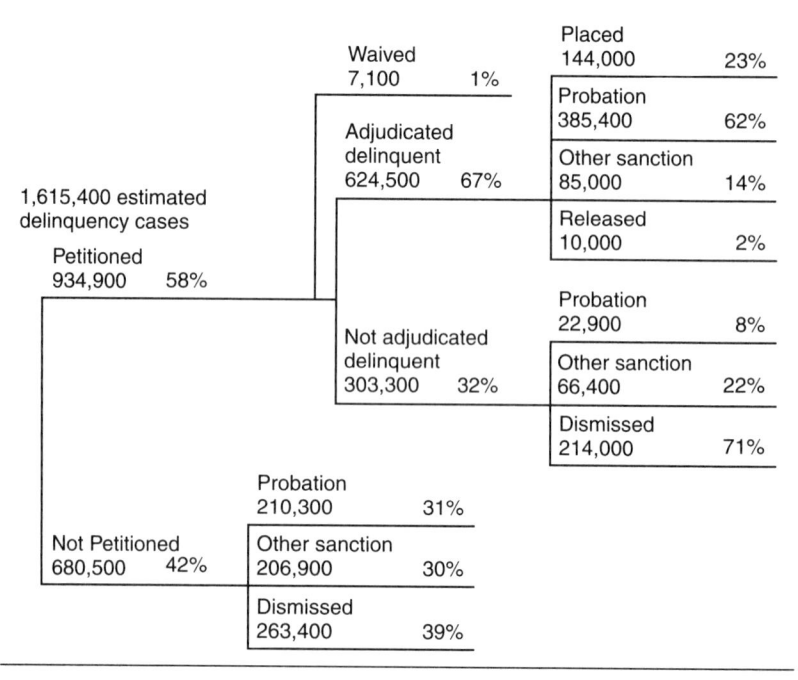

```
                                            Placed
                              Waived        144,000      23%
                              7,100   1%    ┌─────────────────┐
                              ┌──────────── │ Probation       │
                              │ Adjudicated │ 385,400     62% │
                              │ delinquent  │ Other sanction  │
1,615,400 estimated           │ 624,500 67% │ 85,000      14% │
delinquency cases             │             │ Released        │
   Petitioned                 │             │ 10,000       2% │
   934,900    58%             │             └─────────────────┘
                              │             ┌─────────────────┐
                              │             │ Probation       │
                              │ Not adjudicated│ 22,900    8% │
                              │ delinquent  │ Other sanction  │
                              │ 303,300 32% │ 66,400      22% │
                                            │ Dismissed       │
                                            │ 214,000     71% │
                                            └─────────────────┘
                 ┌─────────────────┐
                 │ Probation       │
                 │ 210,300    31%  │
   Not Petitioned│ Other sanction  │
   680,500  42%  │ 206,900    30%  │
                 │ Dismissed       │
                 │ 263,400    39%  │
                 └─────────────────┘
```

FIGURE 2.1 DELINQUENCY CASE PROCESSING, 2002

Source: Snyder & Sickmund (2006, p. 177).

time in confinement than their non-transferred, and supposedly less threatening, counterparts. Nationally, rates of waiver remained fairly stable despite legislative changes, hovering at about 1 percent throughout the 1980s and 1990s. Figure 2.1 reports data for 2002. Note that the figures are for actions taken by juvenile courts (while Table 2.1, earlier in the chapter, reported police dispositions). Initial increases in the number of juvenile court cases transferred (waived) to criminal courts—from 8,000 to 12,100 between 1989 and 1994—subsequently declined, further evidence of the importance of *local* conditions and decisions in these matters.

Although relatively few juveniles are waived to criminal courts, the *number* of juveniles under age 18 held in *state prisons* more than doubled between 1985 and 1997, as part of the nation's increasing reliance on incarceration for crime control. Crime rates later dropped,

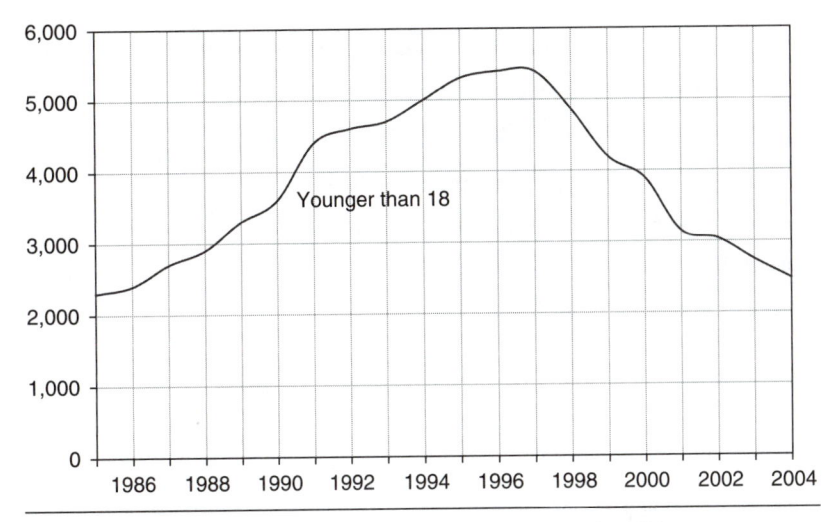

FIGURE 2.2 NUMBER OF JUVENILES HELD IN ADULT STATE PRISONS, 1985–2004

Source: Snyder & Sickmund (2006, p. 238).

but many persons convicted as juveniles remain in prison with sentences of life without parole (see Figure 2.2).

THE "WAR ON DRUGS" AND RACIAL DISPARITIES

The initial surge in juveniles waived to criminal court was part of a larger "war on drugs." In the 1980s, crack cocaine exploded onto the streets of America, wreaking havoc in some communities and destroying many lives. Especially hard hit were predominantly black, inner-city neighborhoods, where crack was cheap, readily available, and a major factor in escalating gun violence. As law enforcement redoubled efforts to stop drug trafficking in these neighborhoods, more and more blacks—adults and youth—were arrested and brought into the system. Once there, they were likely to receive more severe dispositions than whites at almost every stage of processing, which for black youth meant greater rates of detainment, waiver to criminal court, and residential placement for drug and other charges (see Figure 2.3). The cumulative effect of racial disparities at

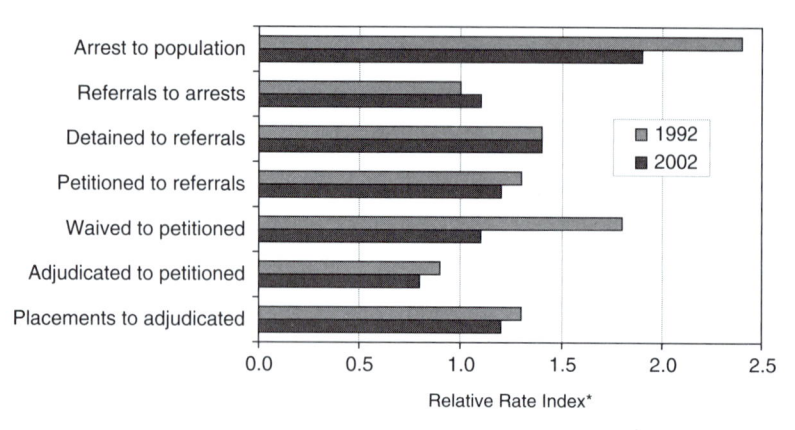

[Chart showing Relative Rate Index for 1992 and 2002 across categories: Arrest to population, Referrals to arrests, Detained to referrals, Petitioned to referrals, Waived to petitioned, Adjudicated to petitioned, Placements to adjudicated]

*The Relative Rate Index (RRI) is computed by dividing the black rate by the white rate. A RRI of 1.0 indicates no racial disparity; a RRI greater than 1.0 indicates that the black rate is higher than the rate for whites.

FIGURE 2.3   RELATIVE RATE INDEX, 1992 AND 2002

Source: Snyder & Sickmund (2006, p. 190).

each decision point was a marked overrepresentation of blacks in secure detention facilities ("disproportionate minority confinement," or DMC).

Although changes in federal legislation appear to have resulted in a decline in DMC, minorities—blacks and, increasingly, Hispanics—continue to be overrepresented in both adult and juvenile justice systems. Research addressing such disparities has been inconsistent, with some studies finding evidence of discrimination based on race or ethnicity while others report that disparities disappear once legal factors (offense severity and prior record) are taken into account. Again, however, context is important.

Institutional discrimination continues to be a major problem in American society. As an example, the 1986 Anti-Drug Abuse Act, passed during the height of the panic surrounding crack cocaine, increased the penalty for possession or distribution of five grams of *crack cocaine* to a mandatory five-year prison sentence without the possibility of parole, one hundred times the penalty for *powdered* cocaine, the form generally preferred by whites. Under this law, thousands of blacks—mostly males—were sent to federal prison on convictions for crack cocaine offenses, and many more were incarcerated by states following the federal trends. The effects on the families, children, and communities were often devastating.

Again, politics interfered with attempts to rectify this situation. Despite the U.S. Sentencing Commission's recommendation that the legal distinction between crack and powdered forms of cocaine be dropped and that the penalty for possession of 100 grams of either be the same (one year in prison), the effort failed. The head of the National Legal Aid and Defender Association noted that it was difficult for lawmakers to make the change as they headed into an election year (Clear, Cole, & Reisig, 2006, p. 91).

INTO THE NEW MILLENNIUM

The U.S. Supreme Court also supported "get tough" laws passed by the states, from confidentiality issues to the death penalty.[3] Nevertheless, the Court has never abandoned the logic of separate juvenile and adult justice systems. Vestiges of the reformist past have continued to be quite evident, especially in cases involving capital punishment. In *Eddings v. Oklahoma* (1982), for example, the Court ruled that the age of the defendant must be considered a mitigating factor in death penalty cases. Six years later, in *Thompson v. Oklahoma* (1988), the Court held that the Eighth and Fourteenth Amendments to the Constitution prohibit states without a statutorily defined minimum age limit from executing someone who was under age 16 at the time of the crime. And on March 1, 2005, the Court banned the imposition of the death penalty for juveniles, ruling by a 5 to 4 vote in *Roper v. Simmons* that the Eighth and Fourteenth Amendments forbid states from executing a defendant under age 18 at the time of the crime. Likening the practice to capital punishment for mentally retarded persons, the Court concluded that it raises serious culpability issues and stands in stark contrast to "evolving standards of decency that mark the progress of a maturing society." Prior to this ruling, only 15 states explicitly proscribed the execution of anyone under age 18 when the crime had been committed.

We must keep in mind that the Court is largely a reactive institution, intervening and shaping public policy only when solicited by others. Much of what transpires in our systems of justice is a function of state-level decision making. As we begin the new millennium, states are experiencing pressure from all sides to change the way they do business. Many have thrown their support behind community policing, a problem-solving and proactive approach that first took hold in the 1980s. Some have also begun to address racial and gender disparities in arrests and delinquency case processing, as well as the widespread issue of DMC. Additionally, in response to problems of overcrowding and soaring costs, more and more states are scaling back their efforts to crack down on drug offenders and offenses. The implications of all of these trends for the juvenile court system are unclear, but we can be certain that they will raise new questions and force new answers. As in the past, the greatest challenge facing juvenile courts remains the tension between continuity and change, that is, between early reformist ideals and efforts to "make the juvenile court more like a criminal court" (Bernard, 2006, p. 3).

NOTES

1. *Gault* also removed all doubt as to whether the earlier holding extended to jurisdictions outside of the District of Columbia.
2. The OJJDP is the organizational unit within the U.S. Department of Justice that had solicited and funded the assessment.
3. For example, in several major cases, the Court ruled that: preventative detention is permissible for juvenile offenders who appear to be dangerous (*Schall v. Martin*, 1984); executing juveniles who committed their crime at age 16 or 17 does not violate the U.S. Constitution (*Stanford v. Kentucky*, 1989 and *Wilkins v. Missouri*, 1989); and states may not impose criminal sanctions on newspaper agencies for publishing a juvenile delinquent's name (*Smith v. Daily Mail Publishing Co.*, 1979).

3 | STUDYING JUVENILE DELINQUENCY AND JUVENILE DELINQUENTS

Accurate counts of various social phenomena have been important to policy makers and citizens alike since at least early Greek and Roman times. Still, the century just past may well be "the first measured century..."

Mosher, Miethe, & Phillips (2002, p. 56)

The massive social changes that culminated in the establishment of juvenile courts throughout the United States and in many other countries accelerated during the twentieth century. Driven by scientific advances, technologies of transportation and communication changed institutional and organizational life as never before in human history. Among the major changes during that century was the development of sophisticated systems of recording behaviors of interest in education, economic production and consumption, religion, families, and law enforcement. Every domain of the sciences became more specialized and differentiated, and the professions came increasingly to need and use *data*. Although the social and behavioral sciences did not develop as rapidly as the physical and biological sciences, they too became more specialized and scientifically oriented, and they began *systematically*, for the first time, to collect information about human behavior, including crime and criminals, juvenile delinquency and juvenile delinquents. Many of these efforts were supported by agencies of government, including those associated with law enforcement and the administration of justice. The result, as aptly described in the quotation at the beginning of this chapter, is that the twentieth century became "the first measured century" in human history.

Child-rearing practices as well as the behavior of young people, their families, and communities, were profoundly affected by these changes. This chapter only sketches these changes in broad outline, leaving for later chapters discussion of their influence on the social distribution of delinquency and the nature of delinquents and of delinquency in varied social and cultural contexts.

IDENTIFYING DELINQUENTS AND MEASURING DELINQUENCY

A major problem confronting anyone who wants to understand juvenile delinquency is how to study it. In order to do this, we need to know how to measure delinquency and how to identify delinquents. These problems are not as simple as they seem. We can, of course, identify as delinquents the young people who are arrested or those whom the juvenile court identifies as delinquents. But consider the sorts of behavior that are included in legal statutes. Many are not crimes, but behavior problems. Should they, therefore, be ignored? Probably not, if studies of early childhood aggression and other conduct problems are to be believed. But this is getting ahead of our story.

So, how do we measure delinquency and how do we identify delinquents, and how do we go about studying them? The history and the many difficulties of doing so are illustrated by the title of Clayton Mosher and colleagues' book, *The Mismeasure of Crime* (2002). Here we can only describe and briefly evaluate the principal methods used to find answers to such questions.

Official Records

The most common strategy for measuring and identifying delinquents involves use of official records. Nowadays, government agencies routinely report statistics concerning their primary operations and concerns. Some of these agencies are part of the executive or judicial branches of governments at the federal or local levels. Examples include the Bureau of Justice Statistics (BJS), the Bureau of Labor Statistics, the U.S. Census Bureau, and the National Center of Health, which publishes the nation's vital statistics. Researchers interested in crime and juvenile delinquency have relied on data from many such agencies, either alone or in various combinations. However, the most popular sources of official statistics are police and court records.

Police Records. Police records have long been the most widely used crime data in the United States. Every year since 1930, the FBI has compiled crime reports submitted annually by law enforcement agencies throughout the country; today, there are more than 17,000 participating agencies, covering 95 percent of the national population. Intended to enhance law enforcement administration and practice, this data system is known as the Uniform Crime Reports (UCR). It is based on *crimes known to the police*, on the grounds that police reports are closer to the actual commission of crime than any other official action. Initially, the UCR classified offenses according to their severity. The rationale for this "hierarchy rule" was that the most serious offenses were the most likely to be reported accurately and reliably. Seven offenses comprised the upper range (called "Part 1" or "index" crimes): murder and non-negligent manslaughter, forcible rape, robbery, aggravated assault, burglary, larceny-theft, and motor vehicle theft. In 1979, arson was added as the eighth index offense. The FBI has since abandoned the distinction between index and non-index crimes, in effect removing the upward bias caused by lumping the relatively less serious offense of larceny-theft in with the others. All publications now classify the former index offenses as either a "violent crime" or "property crime." Since 1995, the FBI has also published an annual report on hate crimes.

Until the 1980s, the UCR had remained largely unchanged. More recently, the FBI embarked on a massive redesign, involving cooperation with the BJS, the International Association of Chiefs of Police (IACP), and the National Sheriffs' Association (NSA). The product of their efforts is referred to as the National Incident-Based Reporting System (NIBRS). NIBRS, as the name suggests, focuses on crime *incidents*. Whereas the UCR focuses exclusively on arrests, NIBRS includes more detailed information on the circumstances (contexts) in which incidents occur, such as the location of the crime, the offender–victim relationship, characteristics of the offender and the victim, the influence of alcohol and drugs, and the use of weaponry. This is similar to the FBI's Supplementary Homicide Reports (SHR), but includes an expanded range of crimes and allows for multiple offenses per incident, which the UCR's hierarchy rule does not permit.

Court Records. Court records are another key source of data on crime and juvenile delinquency. Although researchers often employ local court records in their studies, national figures have been available for quite some time. Since 1975, the National Center for Juvenile Justice (NCJJ), a research division of the National Council of Juvenile and Family Court Judges, has maintained and expanded the National Juvenile Court Data Archive (NJCDA), a data collection effort begun by the federal government in 1926. The NJCDA contains over 15 million case records, including demographic information of involved youths, offenses charged, dates of referral, and dispositions. These data form the basis of *Juvenile Court Statistics*, an annual report on juvenile case processing nationwide.

Alternative Data Sources

Researchers have been quite imaginative as they have sought alternative ways of identifying delinquents and measuring delinquency. Some have observed groups such as street gangs first hand in the field or relied on key informants; others have made use of school and hospital records and security files of stores or shopping malls. However, the most common of these alternative methods are what have come to be known as self-reports of delinquency and of victimization.

Self-Reported Delinquency. Self-report studies involve data collected directly from samples of respondents, by means of either written questionnaires or personal interviews. Samples vary in the extent to which they are representative of larger populations, much like public opinion surveys. Respondents are asked a series of questions about their participation in various kinds of delinquency, usually over some time period such as the past year, and other questions of interest. Answers to questions such as "Have you ever smoked marijuana?" and "Have you ever stabbed someone with a knife since you were 10 years old?" provide information about the proportion of respondents who have *participated* in such behavior at some point in their lives, while other questions ask about the frequency of participation.

Most SRD studies are *retrospective* in that they focus on past behaviors, but sometimes respondents are asked to indicate how likely it is that they would participate in particular delinquent acts *prospectively* under certain (hypothetical) conditions. Typically, self-reports of both types follow a *cross-sectional* design; that is, they are carried out at a single point in time and provide a "snapshot" of the overall delinquency picture. A few studies have been *longitudinal*, however, in that they are repeated over varying periods of time. Longitudinal *panel* studies, which are repeated over time and with the might help us understand what happened in the incident. Measures based on all of these sources of data are useful, but we need to be clear about what each is telling us about delinquency and delinquents. Each has advantages and limitations. How do they compare?

The strengths and weaknesses of official data are well known. Police and court records are the most systematically gathered data on juvenile delinquency and the young people who come into contact with agents of the criminal justice system, especially for the most serious offenses. They often provide important insights into the characteristics of offenders beyond data reported to the UCR system, and they are especially useful for analyses of trends over time. They are also relatively easy to access. However, their representativeness is severely limited. Recall that police data cover only a restricted set of offenses *as defined by the law* (remember the gang fighting example); also many offenses such as identity theft and a variety of other white-collar crimes are not included. In addition, the UCR's hierarchy rule requires that only the most serious offense becomes part of such official counts. If, for example, the gang fight also involved an incident of stealing by one of the offenders, that would not be included in the UCR report. Or in the case of an offender forcibly raping and then murdering a young woman, UCR data would indicate only that a murder (but not a rape) occurred. Perhaps most importantly, police and court data inevitably reflect actions of agents and agencies as well as the behaviors of juveniles. Police and judges make decisions about whether to arrest offenders and suspects (how many gang members other than the ten who were arrested also participated in the fight?), and judges made decisions about case dispositions, decisions that may reflect personal as well as official policies and practices. It is also usually impossible to link reported offender characteristics to particular individuals or to distinguish between offenses involving lone offenders and those involving a group of offenders. Typically, each arrest is reported as a separate offense, and offender characteristics are summed across all arrests. Another problem is that official data focus on legal variables and thus do not provide information on other factors that may contribute to delinquency, such as family circumstances, school performance, personality, and so forth. Finally, official data are limited to those delinquency cases that somehow have been brought to the attention of police or courts; by their very nature, they are unable to provide information about the many illegal behaviors that escape formal detection and processing.

To gain insight into the extent of this so-called "dark figure of crime," researchers often turn to SRD studies and victimization studies, both of which suggest that official statistics severely underestimate the extent and the nature of crime. The primary strength of these alternative sources of data is that they go straight to the source, effectively removing the police and other agents of the justice system from the overall picture. They also allow researchers to gather a lot of information and to generalize findings beyond the study sample. Unfortunately, sampling procedures followed in the NCVS exclude child victims and victims without a stable household. Although SRD studies permit more flexibility, the fact that many researchers draw samples from school populations raises questions about the generalizability of findings because school dropouts and other students not in attendance are missing.

Most studies also restrict offense coverage. Whereas victimization studies are limited to offenses involving a victim (who survived and is aware of having been victimized), SRD studies have been criticized for focusing too heavily on trivial offenses. Finally, both types of data are susceptible to errors made by respondents. Respondents may misinterpret questions, exaggerate, lie, "telescope" earlier offenses into the study period, or (for written questionnaires) enter their answers in the wrong places on the form.

Despite their weaknesses, each of these major data sources contributes to what we know about delinquents and delinquency. None is necessarily more reliable or valid than another. As we will see, systematic comparisons between them reveal considerable overlap. By "triangulating" data from different sources, we are able to reach important conclusions regarding rates of offending and the primary correlates of offending.

Much remains to be known, however. Findings diverge with respect to differences in offending between males and females and between racial and ethnic populations, for example, and how these may have changed over time. Such discrepancies remind us that data sources often serve different purposes and thus involve varying strengths and weaknesses. The trick is to recognize these variations and to triangulate whenever possible. *Triangulation* simply refers the use of different methods to examine the same phenomenon, in hope that the advantages of one will overcome the limitations of another.

4 | THE SOCIAL DISTRIBUTION OF DELINQUENCY AND DELINQUENTS

Reliable statistical data are essential for purposes of understanding how phenomena such as juvenile delinquency are distributed among social and spatial categories: how much delinquency there is in different communities and how many delinquents and children in these communities are in need of protection. As we have seen in the previous chapter, such "how much" and "how many" questions require careful attention to the reliability and validity of what is being counted. Our first concern is with the overall distribution of juvenile offending and victimization in the United States, as measured with both official and self-report data. We begin with arrests.

ARRESTS AND ARREST RATES

In 2005, law enforcement made 8,997,831 arrests, of which more than 1.3 million or 15.1 percent were juveniles (under age 18). This represents a considerable drop (20%) since 1996, when there were slightly more than 1.7 million juvenile arrests. While juvenile arrests for violent crimes during this 10-year period decreased by 25 percent, arrests for property crimes decreased by 43 percent. The most impressive decreases occurred among arrests for burglary, larceny-theft, and motor vehicle theft. By comparison, the 25 percent reduction in arrests for arson seems quite small! Of the non-index offenses, the decline ranged from 2 to

52 percent. Only three offense categories were associated with increased arrests of juveniles: other assaults, prostitution/commercialized vice, and disorderly conduct. Altogether, however, these three offenses combined for fewer than 9,000 arrests.

These patterns are part of a decade-long trend in both juvenile and adult arrests. Following a major surge in crime during the 1980s and the first half of the 1990s, crime rates began to drop precipitously. Arrests continued to plummet well into the new millennium, reaching a 30-year low in 2004. Although juvenile arrests for violent crimes increased by 2 percent between 2004 and 2005, it would be premature to conclude that we are at the brink of a crime wave. The truth is that it is too early to know if this increase signals a major shift in trends or only a slight blip in a larger picture of stability or decline.

COURT RECORDS

Only a small portion of the youth population in the United States is referred annually to juvenile courts for delinquency. However, reports from the National Center for Juvenile Justice (NCJJ) confirm the increasing burden on the juvenile court system that occurred during the last quarter of the twentieth century, as discussed in Chapter 2. NCJJ data indicate that the delinquency *case rate* has increased significantly since 1985, from 43.3 cases per 1,000 children aged 10–17 to 53.2 at the start of the new millennium. Despite recent declines, this overall rate more than doubled during the latter half of the twentieth century. The total number of delinquency cases disposed of in 2003 was 1,628,800, up from 1.1 million in 1985 and exceeding the number of cases in the late 1950s by more than a million!

Reflecting the shift away from the *parens patriae* doctrine, the number of cases handled *informally* by the courts has decreased significantly since the early years of the "get tough" era. Approximately

> Child protection agencies provide a safety net for abused and neglected children and those at risk of maltreatment. In 2004, using more than $23 billion, they fielded about three million reports of possible maltreatment, substantiated that 872,000 children were victims of abuse and neglect, and aided 518,000 in foster care. (The Urban Institute, *Thursday's Child* forum, June 8, 2006.)

57 percent of all delinquency cases referred to juvenile court in 2003 were handled *formally* (i.e., with a formal petition and hearing), compared with just 45 percent in 1985. Although petitions alleging property offenses consistently have been the largest single category for referral, comprising 38 percent of all referrals, the growth in the property offense caseload peaked in 1996 and has since declined. Person and public order offenses, such as obstruction of justice and disorderly conduct, accounted for the bulk of the growth in delinquency cases handled by the courts between 1985 and 2000. Together, they comprised 51 percent of the delinquency caseload in 2003, a marked increase over their combined total of 33 percent in 1985. The proportion of drug offenses nearly doubled, from 6 to 11.6 percent, during the same period.

The huge expenditures associated with the broader child protection mandate of juvenile courts are well illustrated in the boxed text above. Reliable national estimates of dependency, abuse, and neglect cases handled by juvenile courts are not available, but data from the Census of Juveniles in Residential Placement show that youth referred to the courts for abuse, neglect, emotional disturbance, or mental retardation accounted for fewer than one in five residents of juvenile custody facilities throughout the country in 1999. Status offenders (adjudicated for behavior that when committed by adults are not crimes) constitute an even smaller proportion, down from 5 percent in

TABLE 4.1 ADJUDICATED STATUS OFFENSE CASES RECEIVING DISPOSITION, 1985–2002

Offense	Residential Placement (%)	Formal Probation (%)
Runaway	27	61
Truancy	11	78
Ungovernability	26	66
Liquor	8	57

Source: Snyder & Sickmund (2006, p. 191).

1997 to 4 percent in 1999. Analyses of a sample of adjudicated status offense cases between 1985 and 2002 reveal that juvenile courts ordered probation for status offenders far more often than residential placement (Table 4.1).

As noted in Chapter 2, the reluctance of juvenile courts to order incarceration in status offense cases can be traced to the Juvenile Justice and Delinquency Prevention Act of 1974, which elevated the deinstitutionalization of status offenders to a high priority within the juvenile justice system. The tendency to view and treat status offenders differently is also reflected, and perhaps shaped, by the handling of their cases prior to adjudication. In contrast to delinquency cases, police generally are not the primary source of referral to the courts in status offense cases. The one exception involves liquor law violations, which include minors in possession of alcohol. Moreover, only a small proportion of juveniles involved in status offense cases are detained prior to adjudication in the courts (Table 4.2).

SELF-REPORTS OF DELINQUENCY

From self-reported delinquency (SRD) studies, we know that participation in delinquent behavior at some point in the past three or more years is nearly universal among youth. In a given year, however, serious delinquent behavior tends to be a relatively rare event. Data from the

TABLE 4.2 PETITIONED STATUS OFFENSE CASES DETAINED, 1985–2002

Most Serious Offense	%
All status offenses	9
Runaway	16
Truancy	4
Ungovernability	10
Liquor	8

Source: Stahl et al. (2005, p. 68).

National Longitudinal Survey of Youth 1997 (NLSY97) reveal that less than 5 percent of all surveyed 12-year-olds self-reported selling drugs or stealing something worth more than $50. Fewer than one in ten of these youth self-reported using marijuana, running away from home, or carrying a handgun. Assault and property destruction were more common, as were use of cigarettes and alcohol. Even so, most youth did not report engaging in such behaviors. Instead, at least for drugs and alcohol, the data suggest that the minority of youth who report alcohol use within the past 30 days tend to be the same youth who report other substance use behaviors (Figure 4.1).

Data from Monitoring the Future (MTF) also reveal low 12-month prevalence rates among high school seniors. Between 1991 and 2003, the majority of these youth reported little to no involvement in most types of delinquent and deviant behaviors. However, alcohol and marijuana/hashish continue to be significant problems despite recent declines in self-reported use. Alcohol clearly is the drug of choice among most people, young and old. Of surveyed youth, 70.1 percent reported using alcohol at some point in the previous 12 months; 34.9 percent reported using marijuana/hashish. Shoplifting, stealing something worth under $50, trespassing, and fighting were self-reported by approximately one-fifth to a quarter of

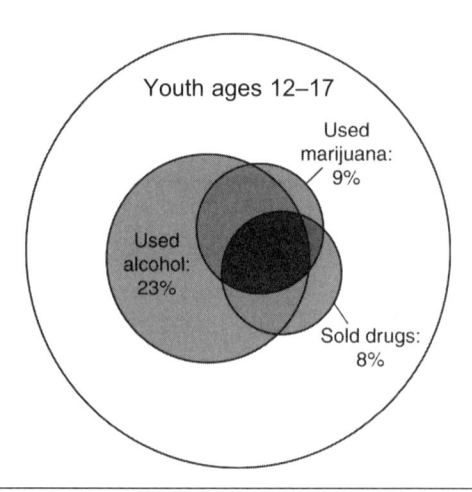

FIGURE 4.1 CO-OCCURRENCE OF SUBSTANCE USE WITHIN THE PAST 30 DAYS AMONG YOUTH AGED 12–17

Source: Snyder & Sickmund (2006, p. 81).

surveyed youth. Reflecting typical adolescent behavior, nearly nine in ten reported arguing or fighting with one or both of their parents.

VICTIMIZATION

Both fatal and non-fatal violent victimization of juveniles continue to be serious problems in the United States. Despite substantial decreases between 1993 and 2003, for example, homicide remains as one of the leading causes of death for persons aged 18 and under. Compared with adults, juveniles also are more likely to be the victims of robbery, aggravated assault, rape or sexual assault, and simple assault. Contrary to popular images of criminals as strangers, the perpetrators of violence against juveniles typically are known to the youth (i.e., family members or acquaintances); with the exception of robbery, rarely is the offender reported to be a stranger. Although schools are among the most common settings for violent victimizations, the rate of non-fatal violent crimes both away from and in school has decreased. Rates of school murders involving one victim have also dropped since the early 1990s, and the risk of a juvenile being killed in school remains very low. Perhaps as a result of copycat phenomena spawned by extensive media coverage of the Columbine massacre and other similar events, however, school shootings in which multiple juveniles are killed have increased. Still, less than 1 percent of all students aged 12–18 reported being the victim of a serious violent crime in 2003. Students more often reported bullying, verbal harassment, or the presence of gangs and hate-related graffiti in school.

THE SOCIAL DISTRIBUTION OF JUVENILE DELINQUENCY

The social distribution of delinquency and delinquents is important for both public and scientific understanding, which in turn influences social control policies and practices. Importantly, however, we want to know more about such distributions than can be gleaned from simple counts and rates. Here we return to the *context* problem. Are there special contexts that help to explain how juvenile delinquency is distributed?

Delinquent behavior, like all social problems (including adult crime), is not distributed equally among social categories. The extent to which young people become involved in delinquency varies according to their age, gender, and race/ethnicity, as well their social class, place of residence, and other aspects of life. The relationships between delinquency and some of these characteristics have been confirmed so many times and in many different places that they are referred to as "correlates of crime/delinquency," "facts a theory must fit," or "empirical regularities." Yet, as we shall see, official and unofficial measures do not always agree.

Age

One of the most well-established empirical regularities is the distribution of crime and delinquent behavior by age. Generally speaking, involvement in serious delinquent and criminal behavior begins to increase during the early teenage years, peaks during late adolescence and young adulthood, and declines steadily thereafter. Although there are variations by type of offense, with some offenses having a later starting and/or ending point, the shape of the relationship between age and most offenses resembles an "inverted j" when plotted on a graph.

To get a sense of the offending patterns of youth in differing age categories, researchers typically examine age-specific arrest rates (the number of arrests per 100,000 population in a specific age group), which permit comparisons across groups of unequal size (Figure 4.2). Note that peak involvement in burglary and robbery occurs at age 17, but the burglary rate declines more rapidly than robbery, and the aggravated assault rate both peaks and falls to one-half of its peak much later in life. Another way to look at the age-specific pattern of offending is revealed in Table 4.3. For both property and violent offenses, age-specific arrest rates are much higher among 13- and 14-year-olds than among younger children, and they tend to increase for each subsequent age category throughout the teen years. For example, in 2001, the age-specific homicide rate for youth under age 12 was 0.1, compared with 9.4 for 16-year-olds and 16.8 for 17-year-olds.

Court data reveal a similar pattern, showing that the delinquency case rate increases with the age of the referred juvenile. In 2002, for example, the age-specific case rate for 17-year-olds was 109.1, compared with just 4.6 for youth aged 10. Although the difference between younger and older juveniles is greatest for drug offenses, the upward trend can be seen across all major offense categories (Figure 4.3).

Youth who self-report frequent involvement in serious delinquency are more likely than their less active counterparts to be defined officially as delinquents. However, both SRD studies and victimization data indicate that official records underestimate the proportion of juveniles

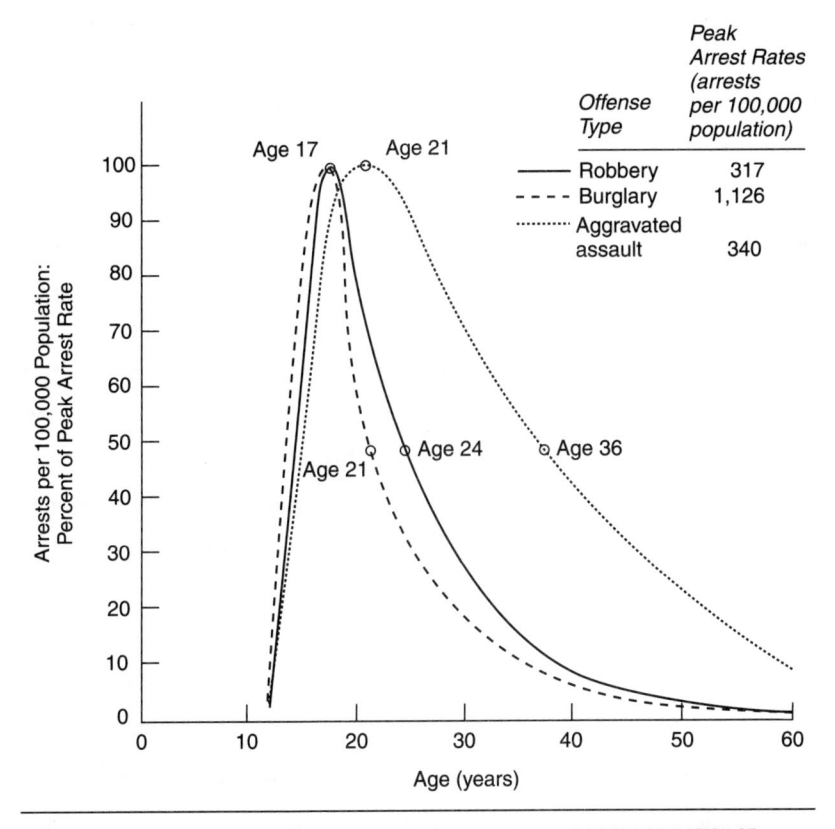

FIGURE 4.2 1983 U.S. AGE-SPECIFIC ARREST RATES (ARRESTS PER 100,000 POPULATION OF EACH AGE)

The curve for each offense type is displayed as a percentage of the peak arrest rate. The curves show the age at which the peak occurs (at 100%) and the age at which the rate falls to 50 percent of the peak rate.

Source: Blumstein, Cohen, Roth, & Visher (1986, p. 23). Reprinted with permission from National Academy of Sciences, Courtesy of the National Academies Press, Washington, D.C.

involved in delinquent behavior. Victims of violent crime (both adults and juveniles) report that nearly 25 percent of their attackers are younger than 18 years, with approximately half of these between the ages of 15 and 17.

Because representative samples of adults have not been studied by means of self-reports, it is difficult to compare youth versus adult involvement in crime in the general population. Nonetheless, self-report studies conducted over the years suggest that juveniles are

TABLE 4.3 AGE-SPECIFIC ARREST RATES, 2001

Age Group	Violent	Property	Homicide
12 and under	19.8	105.1	0.1
13–14	293.3	1,511.5	1.7
15	476.9	2,277.6	4.8
16	582.3	2,556.0	9.4
17	662.1	2,591.5	16.8

Source: Adapted from Federal Bureau of Investigation (2003, pp. 6, 8, and 16).

responsible for a large share of crime in this country. The good news is that most of the youth who admit to committing delinquency at ages 16–19 do not continue offending into adulthood (Table 4.4).

Gender

Of all the correlates of crime and delinquency, none is as consistently differentiating as gender. All sources of data agree that higher proportions of males than females are involved in delinquent behavior and that gender differences are greater for serious than for less serious

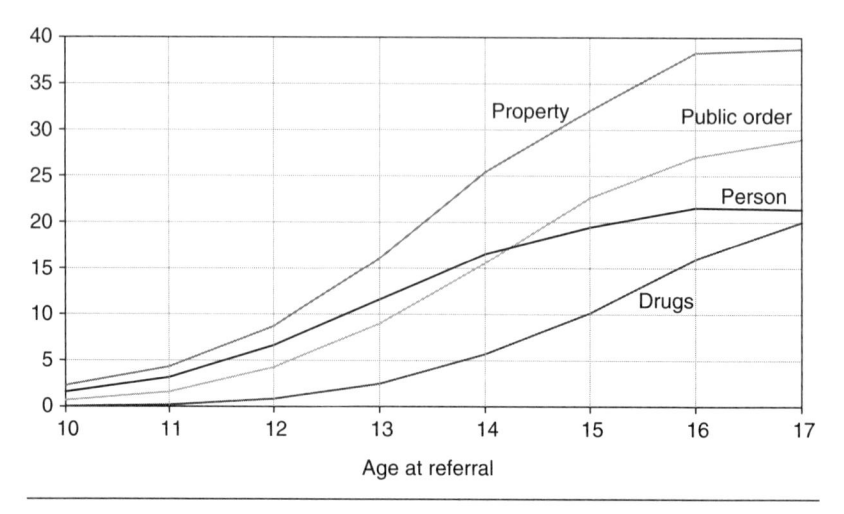

FIGURE 4.3   CASE RATES BY AGE AT REFERRAL, 2002

Source: Snyder & Sickmund (2006, p. 166).

TABLE 4.4 SELF-REPORTED OFFENDING AT AGES 16–17 AND 18–19[a]

Behavior	Only at Ages 16–17	In Both Age groups	Only at Ages 18–19
Vandalized	57	24	20
Theft less than $50	58	23	19
Theft more than $50	57	14	29
Assaulted to seriously hurt	46	27	26
Sold drugs	40	29	31
Carried a handgun	46	24	30

[a] Of all youth reporting the behavior at ages 16–19, the percent reporting.

Source: Adapted from Snyder & Sickmund (2006, p. 71).

offenses. Partly because of the relatively low rate of offending among females, studies of juvenile delinquents and delinquencies traditionally have focused far more attention on boys than girls. Yet it is just as important to understand why girls generally do not commit as much crime as boys, as well as why gender ratios in crime and delinquency vary across offenses.

Arrest data reveal major gender differences in delinquent behaviors, especially the more serious types. Table 4.5 presents data from the 2005 Uniform Crime Reports. For virtually every offense, the male percentage of arrests is much higher than the female percentage. Among the most serious (Part I) offenses, female involvement is highest for larceny-theft, mainly because of the inclusion of shoplifting in this category. Offenses for which arrests of girls surpass that of boys are the "traditional" female offenses, such as prostitution and running away from home.

Although trends in the distribution of arrests by gender have remained fairly stable over time, recent data suggest a narrowing of gender differences in crime among juveniles. Primarily because of the

TABLE 4.5 ARRESTS OF JUVENILES UNDER AGE 18 BY SEX, 2005

Offense Charged	Male 2005	%	Female 2005	%
Total[a]	**949,070**	**69.8**	**411,571**	**30.2**
Murder and non-negligent manslaughter	638	89.7	73	10.3
Forcible rape	2,382	97.9	52	2.1
Robbery	14,264	90.8	1,449	9.2
Aggravated assault	28,311	76.5	8,684	23.5
Burglary	44,861	88.4	5,895	11.6
Larceny-theft	115,818	57.7	85,048	42.3
Motor vehicle theft	16,279	81.6	3,681	18.4
Arson	4,545	87.0	677	13.0
Violent crime[b]	45,595	81.6	10,258	18.4
Property crime[b]	181,503	65.6	95,301	34.4
Other assaults	106,036	66.7	52,855	33.3
Forgery and counterfeiting	1,885	67.5	907	32.5
Fraud	3,176	63.6	1,815	36.4
Embezzlement	450	56.5	347	43.5
Stolen property: buying, receiving, possessing	12,143	83.0	2,492	17.0
Vandalism	58,543	86.1	9,467	13.9
Weapons: carrying, possessing, etc.	24,148	89.9	2,711	10.1
Prostitution and commercialized vice	169	22.3	590	77.7
Sex offenses (except forcible rape and prostitution)	9,696	91.7	877	8.3
Drug abuse violations	93,769	81.6	21,119	18.4
Gambling	381	95.7	17	4.3
Offenses against the family and children	2,076	59.9	1,387	40.1
Driving under the influence	9,192	77.7	2,632	22.3
Liquor laws	55,239	64.0	31,089	36.0

(*continued*)

Offense Charged	Male 2005	%	Female 2005	%
Drunkenness	8,063	76.2	2,513	23.8
Disorderly conduct	88,170	67.2	43,004	32.8
Vagrancy	2,298	72.4	875	27.6
All other offenses (except traffic)	172,737	72.2	66,512	27.8
Suspicion	253	75.1	84	24.9
Curfew and loitering law violations	41,889	67.4	20,282	32.6
Runaways	31,912	41.8	44,521	58.2

ᵃ Does not include suspicion.

ᵇ Violent crimes are offenses of murder, forcible rape, robbery, and aggravated assault. Property crimes are offenses of burglary, larceny-theft, motor vehicle theft, and arson.

Source: Adapted from Federal Bureau of Investigation (2005). Crime in the United States 2005. *Uniform Crime Reporting Program*, Table 37 (available online: http://www.fbi.gov/ucr/05cius/data/table_37.html).

rapid decrease in male rates of virtually all types of serious violent crimes during the 1990s, the female proportion of arrests for these offenses nearly doubled between 1980 and 2003 (see Figure 4.4).

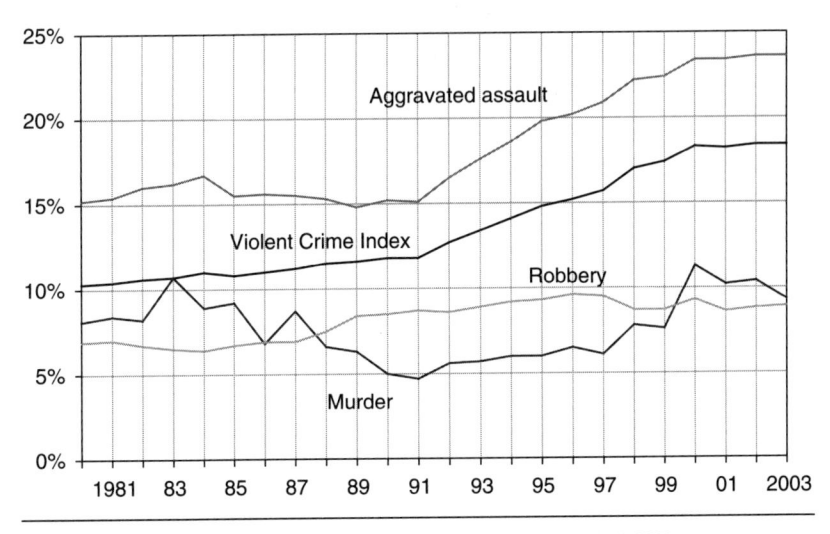

FIGURE 4.4 FEMALE PERCENT OF JUVENILE VIOLENT CRIME ARRESTS, 1980–2003

Source: Snyder & Sickmund (2006, p. 128).

The proportion of arrests of girls for index property crimes also increased during this period, from 19 to 32 percent, again because of faster rates of decline among males. Note that this does not necessarily mean that girls are participating in more crime, especially the more violent types. They still comprise a small portion of the overall crime picture, and observed increases have occurred mainly for less serious, non-index offenses, particularly weapons violations, simple assault, disorderly conduct, curfew, sex offenses, and drug abuse violations.

Likewise, court data show that while delinquency case rates continue to be much higher for males than for females, increases in female rates during the 1990s have been far more dramatic. The result is that the female share of juvenile delinquency cases has grown, from less than one in five (19%) in 1985 to one in four (26%) in 2002. As can be seen in Table 4.6, increases among female cases have been especially pronounced in *person* offense cases, followed by public order offense cases and drug cases. Although property offense cases have remained

TABLE 4.6 OFFENSE PROFILES OF DELINQUENCY CASES BY SEX, 1985 AND 2002

Offense	Male (%)	Female (%)
Delinquency, 2002	100	100
Person	23	26
Property	39	39
Drugs	13	8
Public order	25	27
Delinquency, 1985	100	100
Person	16	16
Property	61	59
Drugs	7	6
Public order	16	19

Source: Adapted from Stahl et al. (2005, p. 13).

relatively high, the *proportion* of cases involving property offenses has dropped markedly for both males and females.

Self-reports confirm the disproportionate criminal involvement of boys compared with girls, both as offenders and victims. Data from the NLSY97 show that, with the exception of running away from home, more boys than girls admitted to ever having participated in nearly all offenses (Table 4.7). Except for shoplifting and alcohol/substance use, however, these data also indicate relatively low prevalence rates for both boys and girls, especially for the more serious offenses.

Self-report data from the MTF study reveal a similar pattern of offending and victimization among high school seniors during the previous 12 months. While males were more likely than females to report involvement in delinquency and victimization experiences, prevalence rates for *both* sexes are quite low for most offenses. According to the National Crime Victimization Survey (NCVS) and data from the FBI's Supplementary Homicide Reports (Figure 4.5), rates of serious violent victimization among both male and female youth decreased sharply between 1993 and 2003, but until 2003 the drop in male victimization was especially pronounced.

Race and Ethnicity

The distribution of crime and delinquency by race and ethnicity is especially important because race and ethnic relationships are involved in so many aspects of social life, historically, today, and for the foreseeable future. Although the Irish and later immigrant groups (e.g., Italians and Poles) were the primary focus of ethnic tensions in the early history of the United States, slavery, the Civil War, and post-war reconstruction left scars on race relationships that have yet to heal. What was once perceived (incorrectly) as a problem located primarily in the U.S. South spread rapidly to the rest of the country as large numbers of African

TABLE 4.7 SELF-REPORTED DELINQUENCY BY SEX, 1997

Delinquent Act	Male (%)	Female (%)
Ever smoke cigarettes	40.1	38.4
Ever drink alcohol	43.9	41.9
Ever use marijuana	21.5	18.6
Ever run away from home	10.0	10.9
Ever carried a handgun	15.9	3.0
Ever belonged to a gang	7.0	3.4
Ever purposely destroy property	35.2	18.5
Ever steal anything <$50	36.1	27.5
Ever steal anything >$50	10.1	5.2
Commit other property crimes	13.4	3.2
Attacked to hurt or fight	23.5	12.7
Ever sell drugs	8.5	4.8
Steal <$50 from store	81.8	83.0
Steal purse or wallet (<$50)	5.8	3.7
Entered locked building to steal (<$50)	9.5	4.0
Used weapon to steal (<$50)	2.2	0.74
Steal >$50 from store	65.1	66.5
Steal purse or wallet (>$50)	14.0	9.4
Entered locked building to steal (>$50)	26.0	13.8
Steal vehicle	17.9	16.1
Used weapon to steal (>$50)	7.1	3.1
Sell marijuana	77.1	74.4
Sell hard drugs	37.1	45.4
Arrest illegal/delinquent	10.8	5.4

Source: Authors' analysis of the Bureau of Labor Statistics' *National Longitudinal Survey of Youth 1997* (machine-readable files).

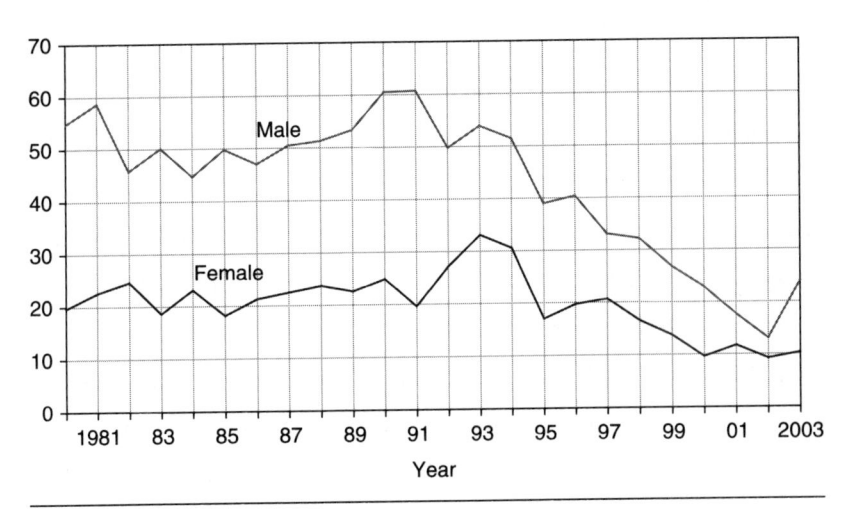

FIGURE 4.5 RATES OF SERIOUS VIOLENT VICTIMIZATION AMONG MALE AND FEMALE JUVENILES AGED 12–17, 1980–2003

Source: Adapted from Snyder & Sickmund (2006, p. 27).

Americans migrated north during the twentieth century. Racial tensions escalated as racial prejudices and practices became institutionalized in many forms, such as "Jim Crow" laws restricting access to public facilities by black citizens and segregated public schools. Although civil rights legislation and court decisions outlawed many discriminatory practices, as noted in Chapter 2, racial tensions came to a head during widespread urban riots of the 1960s and beyond. Rising crime rates in later decades, particularly among young black men, fueled the "get tough on crime" policies discussed in that chapter.

Understanding crime and delinquency among different races and ethnic groups is complicated by difficulties in defining these categories, especially amongst an increasingly diverse and blended population. Another problem is that official and SRD studies have not always agreed. For example, rates of arrest among blacks and whites tend to diverge far more than self-reported differences, suggesting that the police do not treat people of different races equally. Criminologists note, however, SRD studies often do not adequately capture the more serious offenses included in official data, and some evidence suggests that black youth are less likely than their white counterparts to self-report delinquent behavior.

Arrest numbers from the 2005 Uniform Crime Reports show that whites constitute the majority of arrestees under age 18 for virtually every offense. Arrest *rates* tell a very different story. While blacks constitute about 16 percent of the youth population, they make up a much larger share of arrests for virtually every offense type, including murder/non-negligent manslaughter, robbery, and other violent crimes. Native Americans, comprising only 1.4 percent of the general youth population, are especially overrepresented in arrests for alcohol-related offenses and domestic crimes. Compared with their representation in the general youth population (4.4%), Asians are underrepresented in arrest statistics across the board.

Not surprisingly, court data follow racial arrest patterns. Whereas the majority of delinquency cases handled in the year 2000 involved white youth, blacks were heavily overrepresented relative to their proportion in the general youth population. Between 1985 and 2000, the proportion of delinquency cases involving black youth increased from 23 to 26 percent; correspondingly, white involvement decreased from 72 to 68 percent. The delinquency case rate (cases per 1,000 juveniles age 10 and older) for black youth was 95.6 in 2000, roughly twice the rate for white youth (46.3) and nearly three times that of youth of other races (32.5). Although property offense charges continue to be the most common charge for all racial groups, cases involving both white and black youth shifted increasingly toward drug offenses. Person offenses and public order offenses also increased among both groups. For youth of other races, public order cases registered the largest percentage increase, followed in order by person and drug cases.

SRD studies suggest that the disproportionate representation of blacks in official data can be attributed largely to differential behavioral patterns, rather than to police and court biases. Although there are few black–white differences in the *prevalence* of delinquency, data from the NLSY97 and MTF study confirm the overrepresentation of black youth in many offense categories, particularly the most serious types such as assaults and weapons violations (Tables 4.8 and 4.9). A similar pattern is shown for Hispanics. With few exceptions, both Asians and Native Americans are underrepresented relative to their share of the general youth population.

The racial and ethnic characteristics of *victims* closely parallel those of offenders. Black youth report higher victimization rates than their white counterparts, especially for serious violent crimes. Between 1980 and 2003, for example, black youth experienced an average annual violent victimization rate that was about two-thirds higher than the white rate (Figure 4.6).

Data from MTF show fewer white–black differences for less serious offenses, and differences in the victimization experiences of blacks and whites have narrowed over time, largely because of the more rapid decrease in black victimization during the late 1990s. NCVS data show victimization rates to be highest among Native American youth, averaging 159.1 per 1,000 persons aged 12–17 between 1993 and 2000. At the other extreme are Asian youth, whose average annual victimization rate (43.6) is less than half that of Hispanics (90.1), blacks (99.9), and whites (98.0).

Age, Gender, and Race

The combined effect of age, gender, and race on delinquency has generated much interest, particularly following predictions of a coming wave of juvenile "superpredators" (DiIulio, 1996). The term

TABLE 4.8 SELF-REPORTED DELINQUENCY BY RACE AND ETHNICITY, 1997

Delinquent Act	Race (%) White	Black	Native American	Asian	Ethnicity (%) Non-Hispanic	Hispanic
Ever smoke cigarettes	43.3	31.1	39.3	23.8	40.1	36.4
Ever drink alcohol	46.8	35.4	41.0	34.4	43.4	41.2
Ever use marijuana	20.9	17.8	21.3	13.1	20.2	19.7
Ever run away from home	10.4	10.3	18.0	10.6	10.5	10.3
Ever carried a handgun	10.2	8.6	6.6[a]	6.3[a]	9.6	9.5
Ever belonged to a gang	4.1	6.8	3.3	4.4	4.7	7.1
Ever purposely destroy property	28.8	24.9	18.0	23.8	2.8	2.3
Ever steal anything <$50	33.6	28.1	36.1	33.1	32.2	30.2
Ever steal anything >$50	7.4	8.1	9.8	9.4	7.6	7.9
Commit other property crimes	8.7	8.0	11.5	8.1	8.6	7.9
Attacked to hurt or fight	16.3	23.5	27.9	12.5	18.9	16.0
Ever sell drugs	7.6	4.9	8.2	3.1	6.6	6.8
Steal <$50 from store	82.8	79.2	77.3	77.4	82.0	83.3
Steal purse or wallet (<$50)	4.5	5.3	4.6	0.0	4.5	6.3
Entered locked building to steal (<$50)	7.5	6.5	13.6	3.8	6.9	8.2
Used weapon to steal (<$50)	1.1	3.0	0.0	1.9	1.5	1.8
Steal >$50 from store	64.7	60.9	66.7[a]	73.3[a]	64.5	68.5
Steal purse or wallet (>$50)	12.8	8.9	0.0[a]	6.7[a]	10.7	18.7
Entered locked building to steal (>$50)	25.6	15.6	50.0[a]	6.7[a]	21.9	22.0
Steal vehicle	19.1	15.6	0.0[a]	20.0[a]	17.2	18.0
Used weapon to steal (>$50)	3.9	7.3	16.7[a]	6.7[a]	5.2	8.0
Sell marijuana	77.4	70.1	100.0[a]	40.0[a]	77.2	72.7
Sell hard drugs	38.9	37.6	80.0[a]	40.0[a]	38.1	46.9
Arrest illegal/delinquent	7.5	9.7	4.9	5.0	7.9	8.9

[a] Based on 15 or fewer cases.

Source: Authors' analysis of the Bureau of Labor Statistics' *National Longitudinal Survey of Youth 1997* (machine-readable files).

TABLE 4.9 HIGH SCHOOL SENIORS REPORTING INVOLVEMENT IN SELECTED DELINQUENT ACTIVITIES IN THE LAST 12 MONTHS, 1993 AND 2003

	1993		2003	
Delinquent Activity	White (%)	Black (%)	White (%)	Black (%)
Argued or had a fight with either of your parents?	92.3	74.0	93.1	75.7
Hit an instructor or supervisor?	3.1	4.0	2.5	1.5
Gotten into a serious fight in school or at work?	17.2	16.5	12.1	18.4
Taken part in a fight where a group of your friends were against another group?	21.4	24.5	17.8	21.5
Hurt someone badly enough to need bandages or a doctor?	12.5	14.5	10.3	14.5
Used a knife or gun or some other thing (like a club) to get something from a person?	4.0	5.9	2.3	2.8
Taken something not belonging to you worth under $50?	33.9	21.6	26.9	21.2
Taken something not belonging to you worth over $50?	10.8	9.4	8.4	7.0
Taken something from a store without paying for it?	30.6	26.6	23.4	30.3
Taken a car that didn't belong to someone in your family without permission?	5.3	6.6	4.0	5.1
Taken part of a car without permission of the owner?	6.6	7.3	4.3	5.1
Gone into some house or building when you weren't supposed to be there?	27.3	19.5	23.0	19.5
Set fire to someone's property on purpose?	3.3	3.5	3.4	2.7
Damaged school property on purpose?	15.2	10.8	12.7	9.1
Damaged property at work on purpose	6.3	5.8	6.7	4.7
Been arrested or taken to a police station?	9.0	9.5	7.1	8.6

Source: Adapted from Monitoring the Future, 1993, 2003, as presented in Pastore & Maguire (eds.) (2006). *Sourcebook of Criminal Justice Statistics*, Table 3.43 (available online http://www.albany.edu/sourcebook/pdf/t343.pdf).

"superpredator," coined in the early 1990s, was used to describe what appeared to some to be a new breed of young and extremely violent offenders. Although young minority males were never explicitly

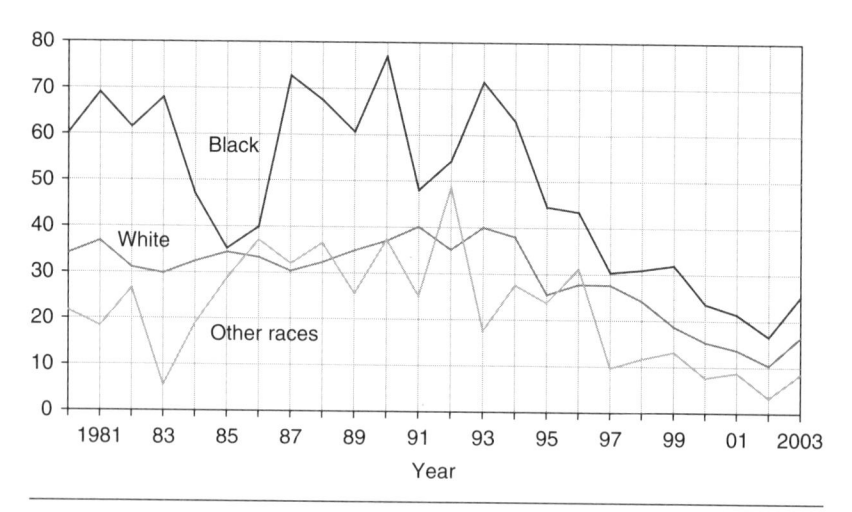

FIGURE 4.6 RATES OF SERIOUS VIOLENT VICTIMIZATION AMONG JUVENILES (AGES 12–17) BY RACE, 1980–2003

Source: Adapted from Snyder & Sickmund (2006, p. 27).

mentioned, the implied connection could hardly be missed. During this period, violent offending and victimization rates were soaring among young men, particularly young black men, and a steady stream of media reports of dangerous "superpredators" convinced many in the general public (and legislators throughout the country) of the need for drastic measures, including laws mandating stiffer penalties for young people convicted of violent offenses and the transfer of these juveniles to adult courts and prisons.

While the effectiveness of these and other recent crime control policies is unclear, rates of violent crime in fact declined dramatically among all population groups after the mid-1990s—so much so that the "superpredator" concept has been all but completely discredited. Compared with non-blacks and females, however, young black males continue to experience high rates of violent offending and victimization. As we shall see in the next chapter, potential explanations of this pattern vary a great deal.

Social Class

In addition to these basic demographic categories, researchers have identified several other correlates of crime and delinquency. Of these, none has received as much scholarly attention as social class. Prior to the development of self-report studies, criminologists had assumed that members of the lower classes were more prone to criminal and delinquent behaviors than were their more affluent counterparts. This assumption was supported by several ecological studies showing rates of delinquency among *communities* to be strongly correlated with various measures of socioeconomic status (SES). Beginning in the 1950s, however, findings from newly popularized self-report studies began to challenge traditional views, revealing only a weak or nonexistent relationship between social class and individual offending. The authors of a comprehensive review of prior research (Tittle & Villemez, 1977; Tittle, Villemez, & Smith, 1978) declared the relationship between social class and crime a myth, and noted that neither official nor self-report data provided much evidence of differences in criminal and delinquent behavior by social class. Although this conclusion did not go unchallenged, the relationship between social class and delinquent behavior continues to be a source of controversy.

Much of the disagreement stems from differences in the measurement of key concepts across studies. While SES is a composite of many things, such as wealth, education, and occupational prestige, only rarely do studies focus on more than one or two of these dimensions. Comparison based on official data pose special problems in that they reflect decisions made by police, complainants, judges, and others in addition to the behaviors of offenders. Studies based on self-report data tend to show that the class–crime connection is much weaker than suggested by official data, particularly for less serious offenses. Self-report studies are also problematic, however, because they focus heavily on trivial offenses of younger populations in institutions such as schools.

THE SPATIAL DISTRIBUTION OF DELINQUENCY

The spatial distribution of delinquency—its ecology—reflects all of these categoric risks. Although urban areas have higher rates of crime and delinquency than smaller places, such as suburban and rural areas, there is much variation among cities of differing size, with the highest rates observed among the largest cities (Table 4.10 and Figure 4.7).

Observation of variations in rates of crime and delinquency *within* cities has been the most venerable and productive focus of ecological research. Some of the earliest scientific studies of crime and delinquency described an uneven distribution of crime and criminals in European cities. In the United States, pioneering studies by Clifford R. Shaw and Henry D. McKay demonstrated a disproportionate concentration of delinquency in "low-income areas near the centers of commerce and heavy industry" in Chicago (1942 [rev. ed., 1969, p. 3]). Studies of urban structure and change revealed that these areas were in transition from residential to commercial and industrial usage. In addition to poverty, they were also characterized by high rates of unemployment, rapid population change, and heterogeneity. Importantly, these "delinquency areas" had high rates of delinquency over time, persisting over "successive invasions of peoples of diverse origin" (p. 161). These findings, later documented in many other cities, suggested strongly that delinquent behaviors were influenced primarily by ecological processes rather than the ethnic or racial characteristics of community residents.

Recent data from Los Angeles confirm the continuing relevance of these ecological processes for understanding crime and delinquency. An

TABLE 4.10 RATE OF ARRESTS (PER 100,000 INHABITANTS) BY CITY SIZE GROUP, 2005

Offense Charged	Total	Group I	Group II	Group III	Group IV	Group V	Group VI
Total Rate of Arrest[a]	5,194.5	5,493.7	5,036.8	4,927.8	4,582.1	4,905.1	6,246.3
Murder/non-negligent manslaughter	5.0	8.6	6.7	3.7	2.9	2.4	2.4
Forcible rape	8.9	10.2	8.9	7.9	7.9	8.0	9.5
Robbery	48.5	79.0	58.6	44.6	33.4	26.6	21.2
Aggravated assault	167.9	226.1	189.9	158.2	130.3	117.7	137.3
Burglary	107.4	113.4	124.6	113.1	88.2	94.3	105.0
Larceny-theft	479.3	444.0	508.7	516.6	485.7	485.7	450.1
Motor vehicle theft	56.5	105.0	57.4	41.0	31.1	30.7	35.8
Arson	5.6	4.8	5.2	6.4	5.7	5.4	7.0
Violent crime[b]	230.2	323.9	264.1	214.4	174.5	154.7	170.4
Property crime[b]	648.8	667.2	696.0	677.1	610.7	616.0	598.0

Total = 10,974 agencies; population 217,722,329; Group I = 54 cities, 250,000 and over; population 38,667,664; Group II = 148 cities, 100,000–249,999; population 22,470,281; Group III = 366 cities, 50,000–99,999; population 25,128,823; Group IV = 640 cities, 25,000–49,999; population 22,131,570; Group V = 1,418 cities, 10,000–24,999; population 22,456,518; Group VI = 5,285 cities, under 10,000; population 17,810,797.

[a] Does not include suspicion.

[b] Violent crimes are offenses of murder, forcible rape, robbery, and aggravated assault. Property crimes are offenses of burglary, larceny-theft, motor vehicle theft, and arson.

Source: Adapted from Federal Bureau of Investigation (2005). Uniform Crime Reporting Program. *Crime in the United States 2005*, Table 31 (available online: http://www.fbi.gov/ucr/05cius/data/table_31.html).

influx of Hispanics into residential communities previously occupied primarily by blacks has led to increased tensions between these populations and to an alarming increase in hate-crimes and youth gang conflict. A Los Angeles civil rights lawyer observed, in 2007, that "in hot spots . . . it is because the demographics are in transition and there is an assertion of power by one group or the other and you get friction." The "groups" consist primarily of youth street gangs. "A 14 percent increase in gang crime last year, at a time when overall violent crime

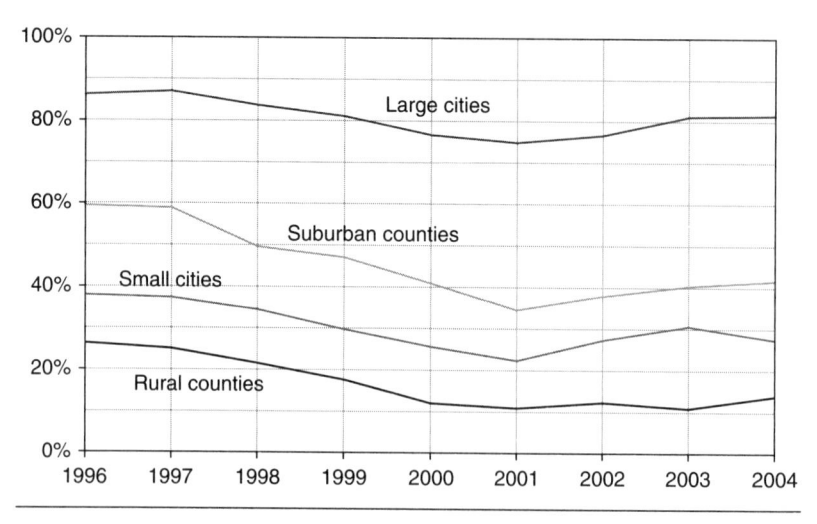

FIGURE 4.7 PREVALENCE OF GANGS BY SIZE OF PLACE, 1996–2004

Source: Snyder & Sickmund (2006, p. 82).

was down, has been attributed in good measure to the interracial conflict" (Archibold, 2007, p. A1). Such conflicts often involve collateral damage, as non-gang residents sometimes are victimized as targets of opportunity. This is especially likely in large cities, where gangs are most prevalent.

In many U.S. cities, the situation is particularly dire for the black ghetto poor, "the truly disadvantaged" (Wilson, 1987). William Julius Wilson argues convincingly that the phenomenon of a permanent "underclass," marginalized by the larger society and characterized by extreme poverty, male joblessness, and a wide range of other mutually reinforcing social barriers and dislocations, has recently emerged in this country. Studies of crime trends in other western countries, such as France and Germany, also have reported high levels of crime and violence among their most marginalized populations, whose experiences are in many ways similar to those of black Americans. We shall have more to say about this topic in the following chapters.

MAKING SENSE OF THESE DATA

At various points throughout history of this country, youth crime has been at the center of what amounted to widespread moral panic. While the early child savers may have been guilty of committing the *innocent youth fallacy* (Felson, 1998, p. 11), it is clear that the problem of juvenile delinquency and delinquents oftentimes is grossly exaggerated. The patterns and trends discussed in this chapter pave the way for more informed understanding and explanation, a complex topic to which we turn next.

5 | EXPLAINING JUVENILE DELINQUENCY AND DELINQUENTS

> ... *the idea of causal analysis is always implicit in the analyst's thinking, for what, after all, is the purpose of a description that does not lead to greater understanding of causal relations?*
>
> Hirschi & Selvin (1967, p. 49)

DESCRIPTION VERSUS THEORY

Facts, no matter how reliable or valid they are, do not "speak for themselves." They do not explain. Rather, they require explanation, and that is what theories are about. Many ideas have been advanced as explanations of the empirical descriptions and regularities that were discussed in the previous chapter.

Scientific theories are distinguished from other types of explanation in several ways, especially in the rigor with which they are derived and stated, and their testability (whether they are *falsifiable*; that is, can they be *proven* wrong). Criminologists have struggled for many years to meet such scientific criteria, with limited success. Rather than laying out details of sometimes-esoteric theories, therefore, this chapter focuses on theoretical *perspectives*. Perspectives differ from theories in that they are not as formally developed or elaborated. Theoretical perspectives are useful guides rather than formal and tested predictors. We will be interested also in the assumptions on which they are based and their evidentiary nature and strength.

Recall that we began this book by explaining the societal and historical contexts of ideas about children and childhood, and about juvenile delinquency and delinquents. Theoretical perspectives seek explanation by examining the sorts of contexts in which young people are most likely to engage in such delinquent behavior. We saw some of that in the previous chapter's discussion of categoric risks of delinquency and its ecology. In this chapter, we shall see a great deal more.

> ... the goal of delinquency research should not be to find the relation between variable X and delinquency, but to learn how and under what conditions variable X does or does not affect delinquency.
> (Hirschi & Selvin, 1967, p. 30)

Studying the conditions under which a variable or a process is associated with delinquent behavior often involves looking at combinations of categoric risks and other correlates of delinquent behavior. The ecological distributions discussed in the previous chapter describe rates of delinquents in spatial contexts, such as degrees of urbanization and, within cities, characteristics of communities.

Other important contexts in which delinquent behavior takes place include peer groups, families, and other organizations and institutions in which children "grow up." Rates of delinquency are high for youth with delinquent peers, for example, and for those who have weak social attachments with conventional institutions, including their families. Youth from broken homes ("broken" by divorce or the absence of a parent) have higher rates of delinquent behavior. But many youth in such families do not become delinquent, and some who grow up in intact families, with both parents, do become delinquent. The difference appears to be accounted for by the *quality* of family life and of parental supervision. Children from happy families in which parents are actively involved in their supervision and in other aspects of their lives are less likely to engage in delinquent behavior, at least in its most serious forms. Conversely, youth from intact but *dysfunctional* families (those that are characterized by constant and unresolved conflict, for example) are at a higher risk to offend.

Even more complexities emerge when we try to relate personality, religiosity, and intelligence to delinquent behavior. Although most personality research has been conducted by psychologists who do not specialize in criminology, theories based on their research have been widely applied to juvenile delinquents and criminals. Early studies revealed few personality differences between offenders and non-offenders, but more recent research suggests that certain personality traits—such as impulsivity, negative affect, and low self-control—are associated with a variety of criminal and delinquent behaviors, especially drug abuse. Low intelligence (as measured by IQ) also has been linked to crime and delinquency, but researchers have struggled to provide a widely accepted explanation of the relationship. Are "dumb criminals" more likely to get caught and therefore to end up in official data? Or are young people with low IQs (compared with their more intelligent peers) more likely to be delinquent because of frustrations they experience in school, perhaps because teachers and others treat them differently? There is also some evidence of an inverse relationship between various measures of religiosity (e.g., church attendance, religious beliefs, fears of damnation, and denominational affiliation) and delinquent behavior, but criminologists have yet to reach a consensus concerning why this should be the case. It is unclear whether religiosity reduces the risk of offending because of religious beliefs about breaking the law, or whether the social bonds that take place in religious settings, time constraints, and other influences account for the finding. It is also possible that people who are less prone to crime and delinquency to begin with are more likely to participate in religious activities.

Questions such as these plague the field. How can we put them together? The empirical observations in the foregoing paragraphs are all attempts to explain by refining and contextualizing what we know about delinquency and delinquents. Their focus is on *individuals*: their age, peer relationships, personalities, etc.; and their social relationships, in peer groups, families, etc. This brings us to the idea *of levels of explanation*.

LEVELS OF EXPLANATION

Clinical psychologists and probation officers who work with children for treatment purposes want to know as much as they can about each individual delinquent in their care or under investigation by the court. But they also want to know about each delinquent's family and community background, and they are always conscious of the age, sex, and race/ethnicity of their charges. Already, therefore, we can see that they are taking into consideration different levels of explanation, that is, individuals and their backgrounds. Similarly, when we want to explain why children behave as they do, we ask about their individual characteristics and their backgrounds that might help to account for their behavior.

The difference between, let us say, probation officers and psychologists who treat or work with delinquents and scientists who study delinquents and delinquency is that the former focus primarily on individual cases while scientists typically study *classes of individuals* with particular characteristics (e.g., the categoric risks we have noted, or personality characteristics) and *classes of background characteristics* (such as types of communities in which delinquents live) in order to generalize about the causes of delinquent behavior. A considerable body of research suggests, for example, that rates of offending are greater among children who act on *impulse*, an individual characteristic. "Impulsiveness is the most crucial personality dimension that predicts offending," conclude David Farrington and Brandon Welsh (2007, p. 48). They go on to note, however, that "a bewildering number" of characteristics are associated with the lack of the ability of people to control their own behavior: "hyperactivity, restlessness, clumsiness, not considering consequences before acting, a poor ability to plan ahead, short time horizons, low self-control, sensation-seeking, risk-taking, and a poor ability to delay gratification"—all of these conditions in addition to impulsiveness! All of these descriptors have something to do with the ways in which people make decisions, and that is an important clue to explanation.

More than a decade ago, a panel of social and behavioral scientists was convened by the U.S. National Research Council to study violence and its prevention. The panel examined many dimensions of personality that have been identified with offending. The panel's summary of risks of violent behavior is reproduced in Table 5.1.

This complex matrix is only a sampling of the many factors and processes that explain violent behavior. How should we deal with such complexity? Theoretical perspectives approach complexity by asking different types of questions. *Individual-level* questions ask how socialization processes and personality characteristics, such as temperament and cognitive ability, and genetic factors lead to delinquent behavior. Note that "impulse," for example, is identified as an activating *individual* (psychosocial) unit of observation and explanation. The matrix divides psychological and biological influences, which tend to

TABLE 5.1 MATRIX FOR ORGANIZING RISK FACTORS FOR VIOLENT BEHAVIOR

	Proximity to Violent Events and Their Consequences		
Unit of Observation and Explanation	Predisposing	Situational	Activating
Social			
Macrosocial	Concentration of poverty	Physical structure	Catalytic social event
	Opportunity structures	Routine activities	
	Decline in social capital	Access: weapons, emergency medical services	
	Oppositional cultures		
	Sex-role socialization		
Microsocial	Community organizations	Proximity of responsible monitors	Participants' communication exchange
	Illegal markets	Participants' social relationships	
	Gangs	Bystanders' activities	
	Family disorganization	Temporary communication impairments	
	Preexisting structures	Weapons: carrying, displaying	
Individual			
Psychosocial	Temperament	Accumulated emotion	Impulse
	Learned social responses	Alcohol/drug consumption	Opportunity recognition

(*continued*)

Proximity to Violent Events and Their Consequences

Unit of Observation and Explanation	Predisposing	Situational	Activating
	Perceptions of rewards/penalties for violence	Sexual arousal	
	Violent deviant sexual preferences	Premeditation	
	Cognitive ability		
	Social, communication skills		
	Self-identification in social hierarchy		
Biological	Neurobiologic[a] "traits"	Transient neurobiologic[a] "states"	Sensory signal-processing errors
	Genetically mediated traits	Acute effects of psychoactive substances	Interictal events
	Chronic use of psychoactive substances or exposure to neurotoxins		

[a] Includes neuroanatomical, neurophysiological, neurochemical, and neuroendocrine. "Traits" describes capacity as determined by status at birth, trauma, and aging processes such as puberty. "States" describes temporary conditions associated with emotions, external stressors, etc.

Source: Reiss & Roth (eds.). (1993, p. 297).

be studied by different types of scientists. The challenge is to relate these to one another and to other types of questions.

The *macrosocial level* asks how background factors such as political and economic conditions and systems, poverty, and sex-role socialization influence behavior. As noted in the previous chapter, Shaw and McKay asked: what sorts of factors and processes account for different *rates* of delinquents in cities, and what other characteristics of areas within cities are related to those rates? Similarly, do the ways in which males and females are reared help to explain their different rates of delinquent behavior?

The matrix also recognizes that different *situations* are involved in macro- and micro-social influences, distinguishing broad overarching influences and those that occur in the immediate situations in which behavior occurs (an encounter between rival gangs on a street corner, for example).

Another way to look at causal influences, and to simplify them, is to reduce the complexity pictured in Table 5.1 to a few elements, as in Figure 5.1.

The arrows in Figure 5.1 indicate primary directions of influence. Thus, *situational* characteristics are influenced by background and psychosocial factors and processes. *Interaction among participants in situations* influences behavior that takes place in different situations. The

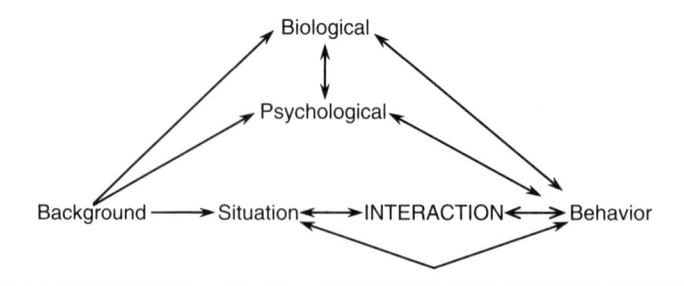

FIGURE 5.1 THE INTERACTIONAL FIELD OF BEHAVIOR

Source: Short (1998, p. 9).

figure illustrates the principle that all human behavior, including delinquent behavior, takes place in a complex *interactional field* of influences.

Note the footnote in Table 5.1 that defines "traits" as *capacity* and "states" as *temporary conditions associated with emotions, external stressors, etc.* All theories that seek to explain behavior assume that all humans have the *capacity* to commit delinquent and criminal acts. They differ in the extent to which they regard the occurrence of such behavior to be *learned, or caused by individual, background, or situational characteristics, or whether they would occur absent control.*

Interaction among participants *in particular situations* is deserving of special attention because behavior does not take place in a social vacuum. Although our behavior is influenced by biological, psychosocial, and background characteristics—and by the objective character of situations—it is not predetermined by these influences. Rather, behavior *emerges from the interaction* of all of these forces and between participants in situations, including how we interpret what is going on in any given situation.

Each of the elements in Figure 5.1 is important and a great deal of data and research, theory and speculation, professional practice, and public policy has been devoted to each of them in the search for explanation and control of delinquent behavior. The remainder of this chapter will review briefly a few of the major explanatory perspectives, saving for Chapter 6 discussion of control.

DEVELOPMENTAL AND LIFE-COURSE PERSPECTIVES

Developmental and life-course perspectives are "especially concerned with documenting and explaining *within-individual* changes in offending throughout life" (Farrington, 2003, p. 221, emphasis added). There are, in fact, many variations within these broad perspectives. Some are based primarily on research and theorizing from only one of the elements in Figure 5.1 while recognizing that other elements also influence individuals who offend. An authoritative (at the time) assessment of the effects of "neurobiologic" traits and processes on behavior more than a decade ago opened with this statement:

> Violence and aggression like all other behaviors are ultimately a function of brain activity. The evolution of brain mechanisms that mediate aggressive and violent behaviors may be traced from humans to other animal species, and most of the neurochemical systems start with genetic instructions, undergo critical maturation periods, and ... *environmental, social, nutritional, and experiential factors modulate these systems continuously.* (Miczek et al., 1994, p. 245, emphasis added)

This statement remains valid, although much subsequent research on human brain development and activity has taken place in the interim. David Farrington, a major contributor to developmental research in criminology, summarizes the "main risk factors for the early onset of offending before age 20" as follows:

> *individual* factors (low intelligence, low school achievement, hyperactivity-impulsiveness and risk-taking, antisocial child behavior, including aggression and bullying), *family* factors (poor parental supervision, harsh discipline and child physical abuse, inconsistent discipline, a cold parental attitude and child neglect, low involvement of parents with children, parental conflict, broken families, criminal parents, delinquent siblings), *socioeconomic* factors (low family income, large family size), *peer* factors (delinquent peers, peer rejection, and low popularity), *school* factors (a high delinquency rate school) and

neighborhood factors (a high crime neighborhood). (Farrington, 2003, pp. 224–5, emphasis added)

Note that these factors are not called *causes*.[1] Farrington proposes a *model* that suggests how these elements relate to one another to cause antisocial behavior, that is, the conditions under which risk factors and processes operate as causes. Examples of each of the elements in Figure 5.1 are included in his model, as they are in the quotation above. Any attempt to explain human behavior is necessarily very complex, and we will not be concerned with the details of Farrington's or other models.

Suffice to say that a key theoretical construct, common to many theories that seek to explain why individuals behave in antisocial or delinquent ways, is "antisocial *potential*." Many theories simply *assume* that all human beings have the potential to be antisocial, but some attempt to account for it. Some propose that its roots are to be found in neurological characteristics and processes, while others regard processes of learning and socialization as critical to its development. The one thing that all perspectives agree on is that we human beings are all *capable* of violent and other antisocial behavior. So how does *potential* become *behavior*? Farrington assumes that antisocial *potential* changes to "antisocial *behavior*" (delinquent behavior for our purposes) through "(thinking and decision-making) processes that take account of opportunities and victims" (2003, p. 231). Later in this chapter, we shall have more to say about learning and other socialization processes that are associated with decision making.

All developmental models recognize the interaction of factors and processes within as well as between the elements sketched in Figure 5.1. They differ in their emphasis on particular elements and in the extent to which they regard behavior as *predictable* or *stable* in response to the changing "environmental, social, nutritional, and experiential factors" noted above. They differ in other ways, as well, but here we focus on only a few issues that seem especially important.

DELINQUENCY, CRIME, AND THE "AMERICAN DREAM"

We humans are remarkably adaptable, as evidenced by our survival under extremely variable conditions and by the amazing variety of societies and cultures that exist on earth. *Within* even the most restrictive societies and cultures, some variation in behavior is permissible, and within highly individualistic societies such as the United States, acceptable limits on behavior are exceptionally broad. Still, there are limits, in law and in the prescriptions and proscriptions of institutions.

All social life is influenced by political, economic, and other social systems and by the organizations and institutions that embody and support them. Recall that in Chapter 4 we described how juvenile delinquency varies in different ecological (community) contexts. Organizations and institutions in local communities are imbedded in larger systems of states, nations, and regions, however, and some exist on a global scale. We will discuss global changes in the final chapter.

Seventy years ago (at the time of this writing), a classic paper by Robert K. Merton identified success—particularly monetary success—as the primary goal of the "American Dream" (Merton, 1957, p. 136, original published in 1937). Noting the well-documented finding that the *means of attaining* success were not equally distributed in this country, he set out to explain the theoretical consequences of the relationship between *the goal of culturally prescribed success* and *institutionally approved means* of attaining success. The latter phrase refers simply to the fact that institutions both prescribe and proscribe permissible means of achieving success.

Merton argued that adherence to the American Dream was problematic for those who lacked the tools and the opportunities for achieving success by virtue of limitations that are often associated with social class, race, and ethnicity. "Within this context," he observed, "Al Capone represents the triumph of amoral intelligence over morally prescribed 'failure,' when the channels of vertical mobility are closed or narrowed *in a society which places a high premium on economic affluence and social ascent for all its members*" (Merton, 1957, p. 146, emphasis in original).[2]

Many elaborations of Merton's influential ideas have been proposed, including a "general strain" variant that identifies stresses associated with many experiences in life as the root of delinquency and crime (Agnew, 1992). As a macro-level perspective, however, the most pertinent for our consideration is Steven Messner and Richard Rosenfeld's "Crime and the American Dream."

Messner and Rosenfeld (2007) emphasize the imbalance in the *institutional structure* of the United States as a major factor in this country's high rates of crime and, by extension, of juvenile delinquency. American culture, they argue, promotes an institutional structure in which *the economy dominates other institutions*, thus exaggerating the goal of economic success and weakening restraints that institutions such as the family, education, and organized religion might seek to impose. This dominance has important implications for crime (Messner & Rosenfeld, 2007, p. 84):

> Given the strong, relentless pressure for everyone to succeed, understood in terms of an inherently elusive monetary goal, people formulate wants and desires that are difficult, if not impossible, to satisfy within the confines of legally permissible behavior. This feature of the American Dream helps explain

criminal behavior with an instrumental character, behavior that offers monetary rewards.

At the same time, the American Dream does not contain within it strong injunctions against substituting more effective, illegitimate means for less effective, legitimate means in the pursuit of monetary success. To the contrary, the distinctive cultural message accompanying the monetary success goal in the American Dream is the devaluation of all but the most technically efficient means. This anomic orientation leads not simply to high levels of crime in general but to especially violent forms of economic crime . . .

How does this overarching perspective on American society apply to the ecological distribution of delinquents? Recall that Shaw and McKay (1942) found that rates of delinquents were highest in communities that were located near the center of Chicago and that these rates declined the farther they were from the center of the city. These high-delinquency areas were also characterized by high rates of poverty, changes in the racial and ethnic characteristics of residents, and population decline, as well as physical deterioration of housing. Research in other cities confirmed these findings, leading to the idea (theory) that such communities lacked the organizational resources to exert effective control over problems such as delinquency and crime. Thus, the theory argued, *social disorganization* in communities was the major cause of the inability of communities to *control* such behavior. The further discovery that most delinquents committed offenses with companions, often as members of gangs, and that organized crime flourished in many of these communities suggested also that crime and delinquency had become traditional in some communities.

As a perspective, social disorganization was powerful, but as a theory it did not really explain *why* social control might be weak in high-delinquency neighborhoods. The *mechanisms* of control—effective or not—were not spelled out. Later research has helped to answer this question. The "systemic model of human ecology" focuses on *networks* of people and organizations and of *interactions* within and between them, and within and beyond neighborhoods to sources of influence and power in communities. This perspective aims to identify mechanisms that account for the ability (or the lack of ability) of a neighborhood "to effectively regulate the nature of the activities that occur within its boundaries" (Bursik, 2000, p. 92).

> Social life is no more . . . than recurrent patterns of action in recurrent structures.
>
> *(Andrew Abbott, 1999, p. 220)*

The "patterning" of action (behavior) referred to in the Abbott quotation occurs to a large extent in *networks* of people interacting with one another. Not all networks are alike, of course. Some are formal, as in relationships that are defined by positions in organizations and institutions (between police and citizens, for example, or the mayor's office); others are informal, as between friends and (sometimes but not always) neighbors. They differ in size (how many), in "the percentage of all possible network ties that actually exist (density)," and the degree to which they provide *links* to the various groups and organizations in a neighborhood, community, city, or other area (their breadth) (Bursik, 2002, p. 74). Why "other area"? Because many linkages in modern society occur across national boundaries, as we shall develop in the final chapter.

Robert Bursik (quoted above) and Harold Grasmick (1993) observed that different networks have different *functions*. Some networks (they call them *private*) integrate people in primary relationships; family, friends, and (again, not always) neighbors come to mind. *Parochial* networks are local. They tend to be less intimate than those that are private but are still important to the social, political, and economic life of communities. A third type consists of *public* networks that "connect local residents to noncommunity-based persons or agencies that control political, economic, and social resources that may be useful for regulatory purposes" (Bursik, 2002, p. 74).

All three types of networks are important to social control: the first because they include family and other types of intimate relationships that do so much to shape the personalities and the capabilities of the very young, and because we depend on them in so many ways; the second because they, too, are involved in the socialization of children (institutions and organizations such as schools, churches, local businesses, and social clubs that are the contexts for much social life); the third because they make possible access to important sources of influence and power.

How do these structural conditions, and networks related to them, influence "growing up" in modern society, and can they help us understand delinquents and delinquency?

"GROWING UP" IN MODERN SOCIETY

> *Kids learn from people they love. If we want young people to develop the social and self-regulating skills they need to thrive, we need to establish stable long-term relationships between love-hungry children and love-producing adults.*
>
> (David Brooks, 2006, p. A27)

This quotation from *New York Times* columnist David Brooks is from a column focused on *human capital*, which includes such resources as education, skills, and talents that enable people to make a living and enjoy life in other ways. Mr. Brooks is trying to understand the income gaps of economic stratification that were observed in Chapter 4, and their association with race, ethnicity, and gender. His argument is that these gaps are due less to prejudice and discrimination than to education, changes in family structure, global low-skill labor availability, and changes in salary structure in the United States ("Employees deemed irreplaceable get big salary raises, while employees deemed . . . [replaceable] . . . do not.") Mr. Brooks' conclusion is that loving relationships between children and adults are the element that is most critical to the development of human capital. His point is well taken, as far as it goes. Loving relationships surely are critical to the socialization of children.

Love is not enough, however. Children, and particularly adolescents, also need relationships with adults that are based less on love than on *relationships* that prepare them for adulthood—relationships in networks that provide support for educational achievement, making vocational choices, getting and keeping jobs, and preparation for stable and nonexploitative sexual relationships—all of the types of *social capital* that are helpful in the often precarious transition from childhood to adolescence and beyond to satisfying and productive adult lives. This is the nature of *social capital*.

Beyond social capital, however, neighborhoods and communities need resources. When Robert Sampson and his colleagues studied a large number of carefully delineated Chicago neighborhoods in the Project on Human Development in Chicago Neighborhoods, they found that three network characteristics were associated with effective control of children and of serious violent crime (Sampson, Morenoff, & Earls, 1999, p. 635, emphasis in original):

1. *intergenerational closure*; the linkage of community residents of all ages with one another, not just within families but between families and among neighbors;

2. *reciprocal local exchange*; the extent to which residents share information and resources related to the control of children;

3. shared expectations for *informal social control and mutual support*; that is, the extent to which residents are willing and capable of *taking action* for child control.

Taken together, these relationships, Sampson (2002, p. 20) argues, constitute "mechanisms of working trust and shared expectations for social control." Sampson and his colleagues call this resource *collective efficacy*, which may or may not involve close personal ties. Effective social control, they argue, is based more on "shared expectations for action among neighbors" than on close personal relationships. Thus, adding to the systemic ecological perspective, "*social networks foster the conditions under which collective efficacy may flourish, but they are not sufficient for the exercise of control*" (Sampson, 2002, p. 220; emphasis in original). Control requires action.

Evidence from Three Comparative Ethnographies

Comparative ethnographies of six Midwest communities in the United States describe "real world" contexts of social capital and collective efficacy and inform their nature and effectiveness (Schwartz, 1987).

"Ribley" v. "Petusa." Ribley, one of two rural communities studied, is a "small world of shared biographies," in which "the foreign, powerful cop and the dangerously unknown troublemaker never confront each other. Young people refer to individual police officers by first name" and "the law stays out of the 'private affairs' of people, even when those affairs would be considered serious crimes elsewhere..." (Schwartz, 1987, p. 39). "In Ribley youthful deviance is treated as 'serious' if its consequences are patently

destructive . . . authority figures define permissible behavior in terms of what Ribley is willing to tolerate . . ." (p. 42).[3] As a community, Ribley valued freedom and personal expressiveness. Differences in behavior were tolerated and authority relations were based on reasonableness. As a result, youth and adult cultures were not alienated from one another.

By contrast, for Petusa adults, community culture was based on order and security as primary values, and as the basis for the exercise of authority. Adults feared new lifestyles and ideologies of the 1960s, attributing them to "the disorder of urban life" (p. 72). Outside influences and internal disturbances alike were opposed with vigilance; peer groups were fragmented, conflicted, and alienated from the adult world.

"Parsons Park" v. "Cambridge," two working-class communities. Parsons Park was located in the path of an invading black population that was moving from the inner city. Residents of Parsons Park were proud of their common heritage but anxious that it might not survive in modern times. Young people resented the fact that adults tended to equate misbehavior and moral corruption. Adult values were not rejected, however, and youth groups had much in common and shared many activities.

Suburban Cambridge adults, strongly focused on wanting their children to get ahead in life, viewed education as the vehicle for social mobility. They resented the middle-class professionals who ran the school, however, and while they demanded harsh policies toward drug use and violence, such policies were resented when their own children were involved. Young people experienced adult authority as "infantilization," and they were aggressively hostile to young people who were compliant with adult authority. A hypersensitive "code of personal honor" often set youth groups against one another (p. 108).

32nd Street v. Glenbar. In both the Mexican-American inner-city community of 32nd Street and the all-white affluent suburb of Glenbar, the tension between "the American dream of success" and participation in "peer group sociability" was writ large, but worked out in quite different ways.

Although young and old in 32nd Street share their rich cultural heritage, life for most youth is oriented primarily to the streets, where a code of personal honor that often results in violence prevails. Intergenerational ties that are the building blocks of social capital are lacking.[4]

The bond between generations is also weak in Glenbar. In contrast to 32nd Street, where "youth do not conform to conventional norms with much consistency because the payoff is so remote and problematic," Glenbar youth conform and avoid serious delinquent behavior "because the payoff is so tangible that it would be foolish to do otherwise" (p. 194). Bonds between youth and adults are weak, however, and bonds among youth are restricted to close friendships rather than organized groups.

Such brief summaries cannot do justice to the richness of these ethnographic accounts. They illustrate very well, however, the extremely varied and complex networks and contexts within which social capital and collective efficacy develop, or fail to develop. And they illuminate the sorts of relationships and realities that undergird the abstractions of social control theory. How do they relate to the individual level of explanation?

MORE ON INDIVIDUAL-LEVEL FACTORS AND PROCESSES

Earlier in this chapter, we noted several correlates and characteristics of delinquency, including the categoric risks identified in Chapter 4 and risk models that focus on such personality characteristics as impulsivity and low self-control. But *why* are young people with these characteristics at higher risk of becoming delinquent? How do they become delinquent? How do children acquire the values that guide decisions about their behavior? What other factors enter into such decisions and behaviors?

Social scientists have a great deal to say about this. Albert Bandura (1986), author of seminal work in this area, notes that we humans possess certain capabilities that, although not as unique as was once thought, nevertheless distinguish us from other animals. Among these is the capacity to use symbols, which is fundamental to complex thinking and decision making, as well as to "self-regulatory" and "self-reflective" behavior. We know that individuals vary a lot in the strength and the exercise of these abilities, and theoretical perspectives differ as to why this is the case.

Self-regulation and reflection have a good deal to do with *self-control*, which evidence suggests is closely related to variations in how *sensitive we are to other people*. The question then becomes, how does sensitivity to others develop? Again, the evidence is strong. Sensitivity to others develops out of *bonds* that we have to those who are important to us: parents and other loved ones, friends, and persons to whom we look for guidance. Research suggests that impulsivity and weak self-control may be linked to a variety of individual biological and psychosocial factors and processes that are listed in Table 5.1. These, in turn, affect each other and are influenced by a variety of background and situational factors and processes that interact in ways that "activate" behavior.

What about values and morality? They are important, of course, especially in such highly individualistic societies such as the United States. In most cases, families are the earliest influences on the acquisition of personal values and moral beliefs; but communities are also important, and community schools, churches, and other organizations not only provide structure for much social life, they also embody and communicate values that sometimes conflict with the values of others in communities, as ethnographic studies demonstrate. Moreover, the acquisition and exercise of moral judgments also involves *interaction with peers*, in friendship groups, many of which occur outside of—and sometimes in opposition to—adult authority. In addition, for a variety of reasons, we do not always behave in ways that even strongly-held values and moral beliefs prescribe. That is why INTERACTION is highlighted in Figure 5.1 and why we return to Abbott's "recurrent patterns of interaction in recurrent structures."

SUBCULTURES, SITUATIONS, AND INTERACTIONS

Earlier in this chapter, we noted some of the macro-level (institutional/organizational, cultural, and community) conditions that are associated with higher rates of delinquency. These broad cultural and structural conditions vary a great deal and change over time, as we have seen. Within them, *subcultures* also vary and change.

The notion of a subculture is straightforward, but understanding how any subculture affects behavior is not. Subcultures are plentiful in pluralistic societies such as the United States.[5] Their attractiveness lies in the fact that they provide special opportunities and contexts for association and interaction among people who share common interests. They help us to understand why members of such categoric risks as age, race/ethnicity, or those who engage in patterns of behavior that set them apart from others (such as delinquent behavior) often have difficulty understanding one another.[6]

The extent to which delinquent behavior is supported by subcultures varies a great deal. Delinquent subcultures tend to be "garden variety," relatively minor and general with regard to behavior that is considered acceptable, required, or unacceptable. Specialization is relatively rare but may be important when organized, for example, around drug use or distribution.

Young people are influenced by a variety of subcultures, some of which promote violence and other types of delinquent behavior. Street gang cultures have diffused widely across the United States and in some other countries, for example, as Malcolm Klein (2007) notes in his book in this Masters Series. Items of clothing, graffiti, and hand signals associated with gangs have become widely known via media portrayals. Youth who know little about such symbols sometimes use them and mimic behavior that they associate with them, in a "wannabe" fashion. They may identify themselves as gangs, and become identified as gangs by others, enhancing their gang status. This is but one form of what has become a cycle of gang and subcultural formation among young people.

Gang subcultures are a small, but important, part of an even more general cultural phenomenon—youth culture—that has been widely diffused throughout much of the world. Macroeconomic and social forces that fail to provide meaningful roles for young people in the adult world separate them from participation in that world. The inevitable result has been a vast gap between generations, and cultural differentiation among the young and between them and their elders. A general principle observed many years ago by Daniel Glaser (1971) is at work here: *social separation creates cultural differentiation.*

The social separation of the young from the generation of their parents (and often from their own parents) accelerated when World War II "baby boomers" reached adolescence. More women had entered the labor force, separating mothers from their children in homes and neighborhoods; adults increasingly worked in organizational settings apart from young people; and more youth sought education and training before entering the labor force. In addition, their sheer numbers became an attractive market for mass media and commercial exploitation. As the separation of adolescents and young adults from their elders across the socioeconomic spectrum increased, their social worlds increasingly diverged from one another. Participation and experimentation with new lifestyles often aggravated older generations and sometimes brought youth into conflict with the law. For less affluent young people, the point of participation in criminal activity, as Mercer Sullivan observed, "is not to lift themselves and/or their families out of the ghetto but to share in the youth culture that is advertised in the mass media and subsidized for middle-class teenagers who attend school by their parents" (1989, p. 249).

Variations among youth subcultures both influence and are influenced by common interests and preferences, in music, interactive media, distinctive types of clothing, and lifestyles, above all, perhaps, in coping with the often-difficult transition from childhood. Ironically, many youth fashions originate in inner-city ghettos and barrios. Youth in more affluent segments of society embrace these fashions, encouraged by media advertising that caters to youthful appetites, fads, and (above all) currency. Youth culture and its many variants thus become major influences in the lives of young people. The socioeconomic cycle is completed when the seductions of commercial products among less affluent youth lead to thefts and assaults that often are associated with acquisition of youth cultural symbols.

Observers of youth groups everywhere note that status differences within and between them tend to be highly refined. They are also extremely variable. The criteria for status within a group, or between one group and another, may be based on relative economic affluence, skills in valued activities, public appearance, school performance, or, perhaps most importantly, lifestyle differences. These bases of stratification typically also become criteria of inclusion and exclusion, which, in turn, create opportunities for both friendship and rejection.

Adolescence is a period of especially intense relationships and shared feelings of friendship, acceptance, and respect. The converse is also true. Feelings of rejection and disrespect also are especially intense among adolescents, and often the basis for group and subcultural formation, including at times groups that are *anti-school and anti-authority*.

As important as these macro-level background influences are—and they are often *very* important—behavior is always to some extent shaped by the particular situations in which it occurs. Although some situations are structured by well-understood rules, laws, and conventions: in court settings, classrooms, and churches, for example; others permit greater freedom of expression and behavior: especially friendship groups and large gatherings.

An example of the latter occurred in the ethnographic account of "Cambridge" (above). The researcher observed heavy consumption of alcohol and other drugs, fighting, and open sexual behavior by Cambridge youth as part of a summer "Saturnalia." "It would never dawn on any of the kids that they are doing anything wrong or illegal," he reported. "It's just like everything is right there for that moment and that's it—I guess abandonment is the word." The significance of such events, he suggested, was in "being together with one's friends in a way that does not enable adults to place restrictions on one's freedom" (Schwartz, 1987, p. 146).

The streets of lower-class inner-city communities also provide "staging areas" where young people gather to see and be seen, and where a "code of the street" places a premium on toughness and bravado (Anderson, 1999). In such situations, delinquent behavior, especially aggressive and violent behavior, typically emerges *in the course of ongoing interaction among participants.* The same pattern has been observed among members of youth street gangs, for whom status threats and disrespect often provoke verbal and physical conflict, inter-gang rivalries, and retaliatory behaviors. As we have shown in our own research (Hughes & Short, 2005, 2007), however, numerous opportunities to resolve disputes peacefully occur in such situations, despite pervasive social pressures favoring violence. Although mediation by third parities, such as street workers or police officers, was the most effective way to defuse violence, we also found that nonviolent dispute resolutions were facilitated by close relationships between disputants, apologies and other aligning actions, reputations for violence, peer backup, and weapons disparities. Such micro-level factors and processes demonstrate the dual character of the code of the street.

A BRIEF DIGRESSION ON SCHOOLS

Next to families, schools provide perhaps the most important institutional contexts for adolescent friendship, achievement, and recognition. Because of this, the school setting, including the journey to and from school, is especially important for much adolescent behavior, including delinquency. This can be seen in variations of juvenile offending on school versus nonschool days, as well as in differences in the daily patterns of offending by youth compared with adults. Figures 5.2 and 5.3 illustrate these trends for violent crime, though drug offenses and weapons law violations also tend to increase steadily from six o'clock in the morning and peak during the after school hours.

On occasion, schools have been the setting for the most extreme forms of violence (e.g., mass killings by students or others alienated from their fellows or from mainstream institutions in general). The specific causes of such extreme alienation are complex, but it appears that schools have been targeted precisely because of their importance in the

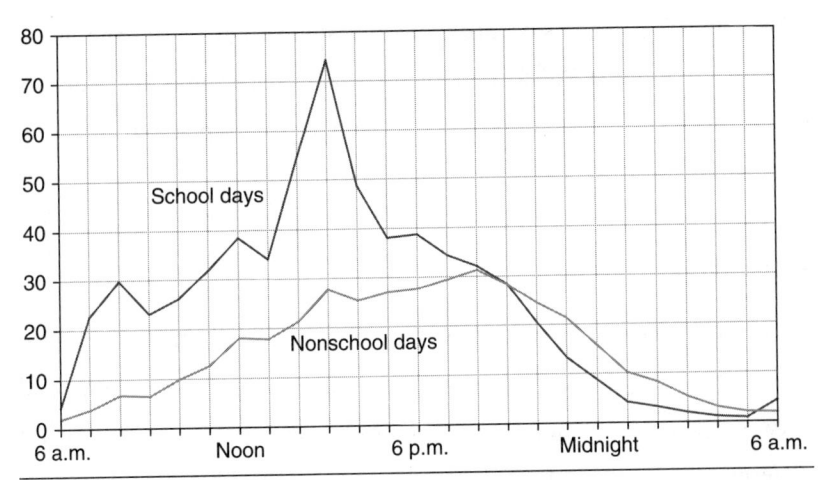

FIGURE 5.2   RATE OF VIOLENT OFFENDING (PER 1,000 JUVENILE VIOLENT OFFENDERS) ON SCHOOL AND NONSCHOOL DAYS, 2001

Source: Adapted from Snyder & Sickmund (2006, p. 85).

lives of adolescents, as symbols of rejection by both peers and an adult world that seems far removed from adolescent concerns. The ready availability of guns at times transforms normal adolescent turmoil and conflict into deadly confrontation. The common denominator of lethal

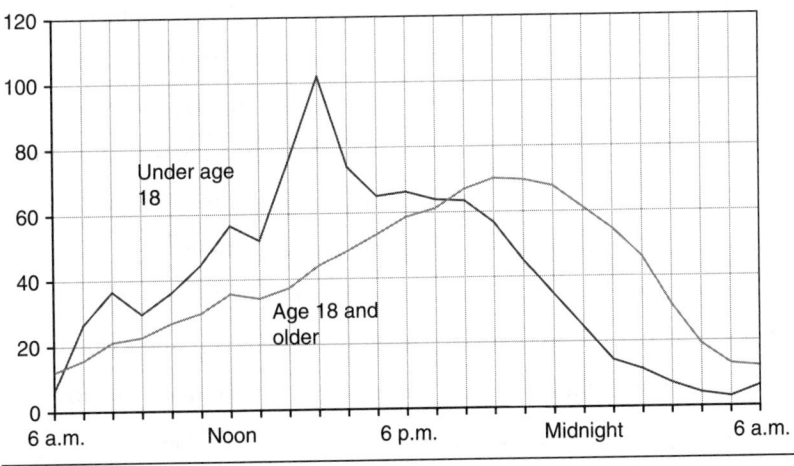

FIGURE 5.3   RATE OF VIOLENT OFFENDING (PER 1,000 VIOLENT CRIME OFFENDERS IN AGE GROUP) AMONG ADULTS AND JUVENILES, 2001

Source: Adaped from Snyder & Sickmund (2006, p. 85).

school violence, such as occurred at Columbine High School and, more recently, at Virginia Polytechnic Institute and State University, appears to be the shooters' acutely-felt rejection by their peers and school authorities.

A FINAL NOTE ON THEORIES

Many questions focus on the extent to which delinquent behavior occurs in recognizable *patterns* that may occur both within and between societies, communities, and other social groupings. Important differences also may be found across individuals. Terrie Moffitt's (1993) taxonomy of juvenile offenders, for example, revealed two different trajectories of offending, one stemming from neurological and childhood problems and persisting over the life course ("persistent offender") and one thought to be much more common and a normal response to the short-lived maturity gap experienced by most adolescents ("adolescent limited" offender).[7] Finally, what about patterns of misbehavior among particular individuals? Do individual delinquents specialize in certain types of misbehavior? The answer, in general, is that most do not. Most delinquents, including those who commit school massacres or otherwise become seriously involved in crime, tend to participate in a "garden variety" of misbehaviors. Some adult criminals become professional specialists or take part in organized crime, and some delinquents "graduate" into these specialties.

Making sense of these and other patterns is the task of theories. That is, theories seek to identify the causes of behavior and explain *why* people behave as they do. Here we can only list the many theories put forth to explain criminal and delinquent behavior (Table 5.2).

Although each of these theories identifies a specific cause or set of causes, most focus only on one level of explanation. Individual-level

TABLE 5.2 THEORIES OF CRIME AND DELINQUENCY

Individual Level	Macro Level
Biological	Anomie
Deterrence	Institutional anomie
Developmental/Life course	Social disorganization
Differential association/Social learning	
Strain/General strain	Interaction/Situational Level
Morality	Social interactionist
Psychological	
Self-control	Multi-level
Self-esteem	Control balance
Social bonding	Routine activities
Rational choice	Shaming
Reactance	Subcultural[a]

[a] Subcultural "theory" consists of several ad hoc explanations that emphasize in varying degrees individual, macro, and interaction/situational factors and processes.

theories, for example, ask what it is about *individuals* that leads to their offending, whether it is a condition or circumstance that interferes with learning conventional values and beliefs or that encourages delinquent behavior, as in differential association. As we have argued here, however, these types of explanations tell us only part of the story. Human behavior, including delinquency, reflects a complex interaction of background, individual, and situational characteristics. To the extent that different theories focus on different parts of this interaction, they will often seem to "talk past each other." If we are to understand and explain juvenile delinquency, bridging this gap must be the first order of business. In *Chaos of Disciplines*, Andrew Abbott (2001, p.117) argues that "social process moves on many levels at once" and at differing speeds; "reality occurs not as time-bounded snapshots within which 'causes' affect one another . . . but as stories, cascades of events. And events in this sense are not single properties, or simple things, but complex conjunctures in which complex actors encounter complex structures." And so it is with society's delinquents and delinquency.

NOTES

1. Careful readers will note, also, that some of these risk factors have been considered grounds for referring children (aggression and bullying) or their parents (harsh discipline and child physical abuse) to the attention of the juvenile court. Although this may appear close to the logical fallacy of explaining by definition (circular reasoning), the difference is that Farrington's objective is to explain early onset of delinquent behavior rather than reasons for court referral.

2. Merton hypothesized a variety of adaptations to the disjunction between culture goals and institutionalized means, including rejection of both, an example of which was "retreatism" into drug use. The "hippie" phenomenon of the 1960s was another.

3. As an example, a police officer told boys who had been picked up for fighting in a nearby town: "If you get into trouble here (that is, in Ribley), we can take care of it, but if you do it out of town, there's nothing we can do" (Schwartz, 1987, p. 42).

4. 32nd Street is the subject of *Honor and the American Dream: Culture and Identity in a Chicano Community*, by Ruth Horowitz (1983). Research conducted a decade earlier, during the 1960s, had documented similarly weak relationships between black gang members and adults "caretakers" (such as teachers and youth workers) and other adults occupying significant roles in their communities.

5. As is true of culture and social life in general, subcultures are adaptive. They change in response to changing technologies and other social changes.

6. Subcultures develop around many interests in addition to delinquent behavior (specialized occupations, for example, and hobbies such as bird-watching and stamp collecting).

7. Laub and Sampson (2003) did not find any such pattern among the juvenile delinquents they studied, beginning in adolescence and extending through the age of 70, thus confirming the complexities and difficulties of identifying universal patterns.

6 | SYSTEMS OF CONTROL AND THE SOCIALIZATION OF CHILDREN

The criminal justice system could be seen as the most dysfunctional of the major institutional accomplishments of the Enlightenment.

John Braithwaite (2005, p. 283)

And so we come to the question of how to control the more serious manifestations of juvenile delinquency and how to take care of children who are identified as in need of the types of services offered by the juvenile justice system. We specify "serious" delinquent behavior for three reasons: (1) criminal behavior, especially that which involves violence or its threat, results in the greatest losses of life and is a major source of fear among citizens; (2) some crime control efforts appear to do more harm than good to offenders, to their victims, and to communities; (3) status offenses and many minor criminal offenses are for most youth a normal part of "growing up" and should be controlled primarily by families and non-justice institutions, as in fact most are.[1]

Again, we turn to history. The advent of juvenile delinquency, separating criminal and juvenile justice systems, came about for a variety of reasons, as we have seen. In order to understand what the juvenile justice system has become and, more importantly, to anticipate what it may be like tomorrow and in the future, it will help to focus first on three questions:

1. What is the relationship between the juvenile and criminal justice systems today? If the criminal justice system is dysfunctional (note the quote at the beginning of this chapter), why is this so, and is the juvenile justice system also dysfunctional?
2. What has been the impact on the juvenile justice system of the theories about juvenile delinquency and delinquents that were discussed in Chapter 5? (The answer, to be developed, is that impacts have been extremely variable.)
3. What are the prospects for effective criminal and juvenile justice systems? (The short answer is that both are dependent on effective community involvement and on national—perhaps international—macro-level forces, as well as local community involvement at all stages of control.)

Just as it was important to study delinquency and delinquents at different levels of explanation, it is important that these questions be addressed at systemic and process levels as well as at levels of individual experiences within juvenile and criminal justice systems.

IS THE CRIMINAL JUSTICE SYSTEM "DYSFUNCTIONAL"?

As we know from the first two chapters of this book, the quotation at the beginning of this chapter was not the first condemnation of the criminal justice system. Two major crime commissions in the United States, reporting in the 1930s and the 1960s, also found much to improve upon.[2] The 1930s commission produced research on juvenile delinquency that has since become classic, including the rich ecological and life history studies conducted by Shaw and McKay and their collaborators at the Illinois Institute for Juvenile Research. Another important impact, however, was on delinquency control.

These studies convinced Clifford Shaw that the primary causes of juvenile delinquency were to be found in local communities and their inability to effectively control such behavior, and, because most delinquent behavior involved young people (mostly boys) acting together, in the group life of boys in local communities. Shaw's solution to these problems—the Chicago Area Project (CAP)—centered on organizing local communities for better control of delinquent behavior and on providing youth activities as alternatives to breaking the law. The core of the CAP was employment of *indigenous* leaders as organizers and providers of youth services in communities with high rates of delinquent behavior. In this respect, the CAP differed greatly from programs that brought professional youth workers from outside these communities to work with young people. We will have more to say about the CAP and other community-oriented delinquency prevention and treatment program later in this chapter.

The immediate impact of the 1960s commission on crime and delinquency control in the United States was greater than that of the earlier commission, in large part because the federal government became a more active participant in law enforcement and in new programs based partly on its recommendations. The Gault decision of the Supreme Court occurred even as the commission was deliberating; federal legislation in support of state and local crime and delinquency control followed soon thereafter. Lloyd Ohlin, a senior staff member of the commission, captured its spirit with the observation that "the necessity to confront the facts of crime and the relative ineffectiveness of the criminal justice system" led a conservatively inclined commission to the conclusion that the system "should be used only as a last resort in the control of undesirable conduct" and that convicted offenders should be diverted "into alternative systems of social control wherever possible" (1975, pp. 104, 109). The commission's recommendations concerning juvenile delinquency and youth crime were even more sweeping, calling for reorganizing "the nation's priorities in dealing with racism, urban development, the structure of ghetto communities, education and family life, recreation and job training, and placement opportunities" (p. 106). Although this sounds like a prescription based in part on the theoretical perspectives developed in the previous chapter, the chief value of "social science facts and theories to the commission," Ohlin argued, "was not to suggest specific actions or programs, but rather broad general strategies for public policy and for reorganizing criminal justice agencies" (p. 109).

Although Ohlin's assessment remains valid, several things have changed. Commission inquiries and recommendations during the 1960s were part of a more activist federal role in addressing a host of issues and problems that began with the great depression of the 1930s. Following the 1960s crime commission, the federal government began actively to provide and fund technical assistance to law enforcement at every level, and to provide funding for research and for treatment and prevention programs, many in the form of "demonstration projects" that included evaluation components. Experimental programs with rigorous evaluations have become increasingly common and have begun to yield an impressive body of knowledge concerning the effectiveness of various interventions by police, courts, correctional institutions, and in communities.[3]

All of this activity profoundly affected law enforcement policies and programs throughout both criminal and juvenile justice systems. Literally hundreds of new treatment and prevention programs have been initiated and many are ongoing. Although few meet rigorous experimental criteria, many are "quasi-experiments" with some type of evaluation. Here we can only briefly describe some of the highlights of these programs and what they tell us about crime and delinquency control.

Before doing so, however, we first look briefly at statistical data concerning recidivism rates as a measure of juvenile justice effectiveness. The 2006 national report of juvenile offenders and victims notes that recidivism rates ("repetition(s) of criminal behavior") "may reflect any number of possible measures—arrest, court referral, conviction, correctional commitment, and correctional status changes within a given period of time" (Snyder & Sickmund, 2006, p. 234). Because national data on recidivism rates are not collected, Snyder and Sickmund compiled data supplied by several states on a variety of measures, here adapted as Table 6.1.

Note that "success," by the criteria in the left-hand columns of Table 6.1, is quite variable, depending on the seriousness of official actions. Nearly 9 of 10 juveniles managed to avoid reincarceration *in the juvenile system only* for a full year following their release from state incarceration, but more than half were rearrested for delinquent or criminal offenses in either the juvenile or adult system. Further analysis, aggregated across all states that reported such data, indicates that the referral rates to juvenile court vary with offender age and the number of prior referrals. "Among juveniles with no prior referrals, 4 in 10 returned to juvenile court but 6 did not. Among juveniles 14 or younger with at least 1 prior referral, more than three-quarters returned to juvenile court" (Snyder & Sickmund, 2006, p. 235).

Crude recidivism data such as these tell us little except that juveniles who are incarcerated in state institutions very often reoffend within a relatively short period of time. More interesting, and more important, are studies of particular treatment and intervention modalities that have been rigorously evaluated, the best of which are experimental in nature. While none of these studies is able to tell us exactly

TABLE 6.1 RATES OF RECIDIVISM AMONG JUVENILES RELEASED FROM STATE INCARCERATION

Recidivism Measured for 12-Month Followup Period	States	Average Rates Across Studies Recidivism (%)	Success (%)
Rearrest			
Delinquent/criminal offenses in the juvenile and adult systems	FL, NY, VA	55	45
Referral to court			
Delinquent/criminal offenses in the juvenile and adult systems	CO, MD	45	55
Reconviction/readjudication			
Delinquent/criminal offenses in the juvenile and adult systems	AK, FL, GA, KY, MD, ND, OK, VA	33	67
Reincarceration/reconfinement			
Delinquent/criminal offenses in the juvenile and adult systems	FL, MD, VA	24	76
All offenses in the juvenile and adult systems	AZ, OH, TX	25	75
Delinquent offenses in the juvenile system only	AR, MO, NM	12	88

Source: Adapted from Snyder & Sickmund (2006, p. 234).

"what works" to prevent crime, they all provide important clues about which strategies are more effective than others.

Crime prevention programs in the United States reflect both the best and worst of public policy. At one extreme is the Scared Straight program, which was first developed by inmates serving life sentences in a New Jersey state prison during the 1970s. Based on deterrence theory, Scared Straight—as its name suggests—used fear and intimidation to induce conformity among youth. After being selected for the program, at-risk and delinquent juveniles were transported to a designated prison facility where they were forced to listen to a handful of lifers challenging them aggressively and telling horrific tales of prison brutality and violence, including "exaggerated stories of rape and murder" (Petrosino, Turpin-Petrosino, & Buehler, 2007, p. 88). Although the rationale behind Scared Straight was widely embraced and spread quickly to numerous facilities throughout the country, it was not long before the scientific community began producing evidence that participation in such programs increased rather than decreased the odds of delinquent behavior. Still, to this day, many policymakers and parents continue to cling to the idea of being able to scare bad and rebellious teens straight.

The results of Scared Straight and other juvenile awareness programs remind us that intervention strategies, no matter how well-intentioned, can raise serious ethical considerations because of their potential for causing more harm than good. Financial costs and the expenditure of other resources (e.g., time and personnel) also must be taken into account and weighed against potential benefits. This is especially the case when accumulating evidence suggests that a particular intervention has little or no real positive effect on crime or on the individuals participating in the program. Among some of the more recent examples of "no difference" interventions are boot camps, which involve an extended period of militaristic training and discipline in lieu of time in a youth or adult prison, and the school-based Drug Abuse and Resistance Education (DARE) anti-drug program. The effect of drug courts for juveniles is unclear, but the success of these treatment-oriented programs may fail to add significantly to existing juvenile court practices, especially if they continue to be oriented primarily to adult offenders.

All of this is not to say that nothing works to prevent crime among youth. In fact, there are a number of institutional and community programs that appear to be quite promising. One example is cognitive-behavioral therapy (CBT), a rehabilitative approach that teaches offenders how to make better decisions by providing them with the skills necessary to manage their anger, recognize problem behaviors and related triggers, and counter antisocial and criminogenic thoughts. The available evidence shows significant reductions in recidivism for participants in CBT, especially when the program is administered to high-risk offenders in a community setting rather than in prison. Modest positive results have also been observed for programs emphasizing early social skills training and for the "school-based, law enforcement officer-instructed classroom curriculum" known as the Gang Resistance Education and Training (GREAT) program. Although GREAT failed to reduce gang involvement and delinquent behavior, researchers credit it for producing "more favorable attitudes from students toward the police and greater awareness of the consequences of gang involvement as indicated by more negative attitudes from students about gangs" (Esbensen, 2004, p. 3). Finally, initial evaluations of the increasingly popular diversionary alternative known as *teen court* suggest that participation in sentencing forums made up by a jury of one's peers may be an effective way to reduce the likelihood of recidivism among young first-time offenders. It might also increase respect for the justice system and operate more efficiently than traditional juvenile courts.

In an effort to assess the extent to which various intervention programs were able to reduce recidivism among *serious* juvenile delinquents, Lipsey, Wilson, and Cothern (2000, p. 5) conducted an extensive meta-analysis of existing studies, with the results shown in Table 6.2.

LEVELS OF INTERVENTION

Note that the studies reviewed above aim at manipulations of factors and processes in order to achieve effects on *individual* offenders and victims. That is, they take as their dependent variable measures of individual offending or individual victimization. The relevance of macro-level phenomena such as those discussed in the previous chapter is derived from

TABLE 6.2   A COMPARISON OF TREATMENT TYPES IN ORDER OF EFFECTIVENESS

Types of Treatment Used With Noninstitutionalized Offenders	Types of Treatment Used With Institutionalized Offenders
Positive effects, consistent evidence	
Individual counseling	Interpersonal skills
Interpersonal skills	Teaching family homes
Behavioral programs	
Positive effects, less consistent evidence	
Multiple services	Behavioral programs
Restitution, probation/parole	Community residential
	Multiple services
Mixed but generally positive Effects, inconsistent evidence	
Employment related	Individual counseling
Academic programs	Guided group counseling
Advocacy/casework	Group counseling
Family counseling	
Group counseling	
Weak or no nffects, inconsistent evidence	
Reduced caseload, probation/parole	Employment related
	Drug abstinence
	Wilderness/challenge
Weak or no effects, consistent evidence	
Wilderness/challenge	Milieu therapy
Early release, probation/parole	
Deterrence programs	
Vocational programs	

Source: Lipsey, Wilson, & Cothern (2000, p. 45).

their influence on individuals. Attention to the manipulation of *macro-level* influences for experimental purposes is quite limited, focused primarily on family and school interventions and on environmental features such as street lighting and closed circuit television surveillance that are easily manipulated. Moreover, attention to *situational and interactional* processes is absent in these efforts, as is consideration of how risk factors for offending relate to one another. The need to better understand the relationship between levels of explanation is suggested in the following summary from Welsh and Farrington (2006, p. 234):

> There is a need for early developmental crime prevention, which aims to influence the scientifically identified risk factors or root causes of delinquency and later criminal offending. Some of the most important risk factors include: growing up in poverty, living in poor housing, inadequate parental supervision and harsh or inconsistent discipline, parental conflict and separation, low intelligence and poor school performance, and a high level of impulsivity and hyperactivity.

This summary expresses the predominant theme and strategy of risk-based experimentation in crime and justice.[4] Macro- and individual-level influences are identified as risk factors, but relationships between them, because they are extremely difficult to specify or to control experimentally, are largely ignored. Although we can readily agree that "promising results of child social skills or social competence training to reduce antisocial behavior and delinquency offers further support for the need for greater investments in early childhood programs" (Welsh & Farrington, 2006, p. 34), the need for better understanding of why and how social skills and competency influence behavior remains. How, for example, do they relate to poverty and family relationships, and to situational variables and processes?[5]

In this regard, Farrington and Welsh (2007, p. 155) observe that because "low family income and economic deprivation are risk factors for delinquency, it might be thought that giving poor families extra money might reduce the delinquency of their children." This idea is rejected on the grounds that large-scale income maintenance experiments did not lower official offending rates of Seattle and Denver children in low-income families that received *extra income*, compared with comparable families in those cities that did not receive income supplements.

Despite a huge volume of research describing the extent and nature of poverty, manipulation of such macro-level forces remains difficult, and findings from this one study should be interpreted cautiously. Moreover, it is important to recognize that the *logic* of levels of explanation applies to the *effects* as well as the levels of the explanatory variables and processes. One of the weaknesses of the income maintenance experiments was that they were of short duration, and by favoring selected experimental families while doing nothing to improve the economic lot of others living in the same impoverished communities, poverty was treated as an individual-level phenomenon. Poverty is no doubt experienced by individuals, but the effects of poverty on communities extend beyond individuals, as a large body of research demonstrates. In addition, as Braithwaite notes, the demoralization of long-term unemployment is especially ruinous in the lives of the children of the unemployed "through the medium of abusive and uncaring parenting by adults who have lost hope" (2002, p. 64).

Recall that *rates of violent offending* in Chicago neighborhoods were the units of analysis in the Project on Human Development in Chicago Neighborhoods research discussed in the previous chapter, and further that *spatial* relationships of neighborhoods were found to influence social capital and collective efficacy for children, providing evidence of macro-level effects beyond effects on particular individuals. "Too often," as Sampson notes, "policies and theories are reductionist in nature, looking only at (or to change) individuals" (2002, p. 227). Neighborhoods that scored high on collective efficacy—collective efficacy defined in terms of intergenerational closure, reciprocated local exchange, and shared expectations for informal social control—had lower rates of violent crime, and neighborhoods that were *close to* high collective efficacy neighborhoods benefited in terms of their own collective efficacy. These findings suggest that both internal community and spatially-contingent mechanisms are at work in controlling crime and delinquency.

> Above and beyond the internal characteristics of neighborhoods themselves—including both wealth and poverty—the potential benefits of social capital and collective efficacy for children are linked to a neighborhood's relative spatial position in the larger city. In particular, collective efficacy for children in surrounding neighborhoods has a direct positive relationship with a given neighborhood's internal collective efficacy, regardless of population composition and a strict set of controls. (Sampson, Morenoff, & Earls, 1999, p. 657)

Situational level and *interaction* must also be considered as important for delinquency control. Our research on disputes involving members of youth gangs found that situational-level processes often trumped macro-level influences in the interaction between gang members and others. Despite the strong emphasis on the ability and willingness—even eagerness—to fight and otherwise behave aggressively that was promoted by the "code of the street" (Anderson, 1999), most disputes involving gang members did not end in violence. Analysis of the data indicated that *interaction* among disputants in the situations in which they were observed was critical to the outcome of disputes. Intervention by "detached workers" and others, including fellow gang members, often permitted, and at times seemed to require, nonviolent dispute resolution (Hughes & Short, 2005).[6] The most successful intervention, by far, was *mediation*, in which a detached worker or another member of the gang intervened and defused a dispute. This behavioral outcome clearly was group-related and not the result solely of the personalities or other characteristics of the individuals involved in the disputes. We observed in our data many such outcomes. We are confident, therefore, that mediation prevented a good deal of violent behavior. Yet we do not know whether or how other behaviors, including delinquent behaviors, by individual disputants were influenced *beyond the situations and interactions that were observed.*[7] It is quite possible that the observed control effect was limited to the situational/interaction context. Studies that have attempted to measure rates of delinquent behavior by members of gangs that have been assigned detached workers have had mixed results.

We will return to the role of different levels of explanation, and particularly to further consideration of social capital and collective efficacy, in delinquency control. But first we turn once more to the juvenile justice system and its relationship with the criminal justice system.

THE "CYCLE OF JUVENILE JUSTICE"

There is continuity as well as change in the history of child saving, from its roots in the nineteenth century through the twentieth and the early years of the new millennium. Throughout this period societies, nations, states, and local communities have struggled with increasingly rapid social change and with a host of social problems, old and new. Among the oldest such problems is the perception, renewed by each generation, that "kids today are no good" (Bernard, 2006, p. 13). Thomas Bernard, citing popular news magazine accounts of increasingly violent youth crime throughout the twentieth century, concludes that despite changes in juvenile crime, both up and down, as best we can determine, perceptions and beliefs that they are worse than in the past remain much the same.

We have seen, in fact, that serious juvenile crime decreased following high levels reached during the early 1990s, only to rise somewhat during the early years of the new millennium. Although most juveniles taken into custody by police continue to be referred to juvenile courts, the percentage referred to criminal or adult courts has risen considerably over the past half-century. And, despite the role of juvenile courts as "back-up" institutions, police referrals to welfare agencies remain at a very low level. Moreover, many studies indicate that welfare and social agencies continue to resist cooperation with juvenile courts and fail to provide services to them. A major assessment of juvenile courts conducted during the 1970s reached the discouraging conclusion that "once children enter the court's orbit, they are less likely to benefit from the services of other youth-serving agencies" than are other children in need (Sarri & Hasenfeld, 1976, p. 42). Why this is the case is the subject of an insightful study of one juvenile justice system. Mark Jacobs' book, *Screwing the System and Making it Work: Juvenile Justice in the No-Fault Society* (1990), is a tale of Herculean efforts to make the system work for particularly difficult cases. Many people were involved: families, judges, case workers, and other agency personnel. At the close of his study, Jacobs speaks eloquently of its failures, locating them in the "overly individualistic conception of social life, the inability to distinguish between public and private spheres of action, and laxity in the rule of law," the combination of which erodes the basis of both individual and institutional *accountability*, the defining characteristics of the "no-fault society" (1990, p. 265).

THE "NO FAULT SOCIETY"

Recall, early in this book, the admonition that because juvenile delinquency and the children who are called delinquents are social problems, *civic engagement* is required if effective solutions are to be found. Jacobs' observation is apposite: "Adolescents stand the best chance of developing healthy selves within communal contexts in which family, civic, and political institutions all nourish each other. Yet whatever social structural causes contribute to delinquency, probation officers can prescribe only personal treatments. This accounts for their recourse to a therapeutic discourse that is exclusively individualistic, devoid of civic consciousness" (1990, p. 266).

The "civic tradition" is also important, Jacobs reminds us, "because it articulates an understanding that the *interdependency of the members of society* is a moral and political relationship" (italics added to original in Sullivan, 1986, p. 184). Yet, now quoting Jacobs (1990, pp. 266–67):

> Not only does an exclusively individualistic discourse confuse attempts to comprehend the nature of children's problems, it constricts the grounds of character judgment which unavoidably inform casework decisions. . . . Ignoring the civic dimension of moral character assigns too much weight in such judgments to situational vagaries, leaving those judgments especially labile.

What is Jacobs saying here? The "civic dimension of moral character" is a reference to macro-level (background) circumstances that shape moral character and inform judgments and behavioral decisions. Juvenile courts, probation officers, and social agencies have little control over such circumstances—compared with the influence of families, peers, and neighbors, as well as teachers and other everyday encounters in organizational and institutional settings. Put another way, individual therapies (virtually the only remedies available to the courts) typically have little control over poverty, unemployment, and dysfunctional families and classrooms. Dispute mediation clearly has limits as well, absent support within other behavioral settings. Interventions at any level are unlikely to be successful without support from other sectors of the interactional field of behavior.

There is, in addition, an implicit moral dimension to all civic matters, whether they involve social control (as is the case with juvenile delinquency and individual delinquents) or matters that on the surface appear only to be about economic and political affairs. Failure to recognize this dimension render unstable ("labile," in the Jacobs quote, above) events and outcomes of individual cases that fail to reform, rehabilitate, or otherwise improve individual lives.

Problems such as these lead some to propose abolishing juvenile courts, folding them back into the criminal justice system, but requiring that youthfulness be incorporated in sentencing policy. Others argue that the system has become increasingly innovative in responding to such problems and that it is returning to the goals that brought it into existence more than a century ago. We cannot in this brief chapter resolve these conflicting views. However, as one knowledgeable and astute observer notes, despite its many problems:[8]

> The evidence shows that juvenile court is the most effective component of the entire juvenile and criminal justice system apparatus. This is true whether one uses the contrasting recidivism rates of juvenile and criminal courts, experimental program outcomes, or practical (everyday) program results as the criteria. (Howell, 2006, p. 750)

The merits of these varied and sometimes conflicting positions deserve more attention than we can give them in this book. Regardless of how they may be resolved, however, all parties to the debate—law enforcement and justice officials as well as researchers and theorists—agree that "a safer, more sustainable society" requires that control measures not be limited to law enforcement and justice system responses "after the fact," that is, after children have been brought into the system (Welsh & Farrington, 2006). So, where do we go from here?

"GROWING UP" IN MODERN SOCIETY (ONE MORE TIME)

Above all, all young people, but especially those who are at risk of violent behavior, need more involvement in their lives by caring adults—not over-controlling, but involvement with nurturance, guidance, and support.

We see this type of involvement in a variety of youth programs. During the late 1950s and early 60s, for example, street workers employed by the YMCA of Metropolitan Chicago made a clear difference in the lives of many gang boys. While helping the boys negotiate adolescence and the social landscape of the ghetto, they served as role models and provided the boys with a positive link to the conventional adult world. Although workers were not the type of indigenous leaders recruited for the CAP, they adapted quickly to the street and were widely accepted in the community. Through their relationships with the boys and others, including the police, they were able to steer these youth toward positive activities and, in the process, prevent a great deal of violence.

> . . . the key public policy nut to crack is the ordering of local knowledge.
>
> (John Braithwaite, 2000, p. 65)

The notion that family, civic, and political institutions need to work together ("nourish each other") is at the heart of the theoretical constructs of social capital, collective efficacy, and the civic dimension in social life. Although effectively cracking the "public policy nut" will require more than local knowledge, it will certainly require that. Too often public policy is enacted by policy "wonks" and professionals without input from those for whom a policy is designed. Both local knowledge and participation must be honored. How much and what type of participation?

A RADICAL PROPOSAL FROM "DOWN UNDER"

Although his target is the criminal justice system, distinguished Australian sociologist John Braithwaite advances a proposal that applies equally well to juvenile justice. Braithwaite proposes a "family model" of justice in which community disapproval is *shaming but not stigmatizing* (1989, 2002). The current state-centered system of justice, he argues, is based on punishment and retribution, to the neglect of informal sanctions from friends, family, and the community. This system encourages offenders and would-be offenders to deny the truth and displace blame. Most importantly, the system fails to motivate acceptance of the active personal responsibility that is necessary if further involvement in misbehavior is to be avoided. Heavy-handed punishment exacerbates distrust of the system and all who are associated with it. The result is a criminal justice system that "deters prevention" rather than crime and criminality (Braithwaite, 2005, p. 282). Braithwaite is not alone in recommending that mean-spirited and punitive approaches be abandoned and replaced by a justice system based primarily on mercy, with incentives for honesty, building trust and reconciliation.

The family model proposed by Braithwaite involves both restorative justice and procedural fairness as an alternative to the "top down" "get tough" model of crime control. A distinguishing feature of such programs is that they are designed to provide offenders with an opportunity to make amends for their crimes and to be successfully reintegrated into the community through gestures of forgiveness by victims, family members, and/or other program participants. The aim is not to force offenders to conform under the threat of punishment, but to motivate them to contribute to community well-being and to avoid causing further harm.

A major strength of Braithwaite's proposal is that it has sparked a great deal of experimentation and real-world application. Literally "dozens of . . . restorative justice programs have been subjected to evaluations of variable rigour that have been more encouraging than discouraging in finding lower criminal reoffending compared to controls" (Braithwaite, 2005, p. 288). While the effectiveness of restorative justice may be expected to vary in specific contexts, the evidence suggests that it reduces offending across a variety of behavioral domains, from school bullying and regulatory noncompliance among nursing homes to property and violent street crimes. Importantly, restorative justice programs involving face-to-face meetings between offenders and victims of violent crime appear to be effective in preventing dispute escalation and retaliatory behavior, and in dispelling distrust and building trust between contending parties.

WHERE DO WE GO FROM HERE?

> . . . the state has no monopoly on justice.
>
> (Stanley Cohen, 1985, p. 256)

We began this chapter by asking three questions about the state of the current system of justice, the impact of theories of juvenile delinquency, and the prospects for effective criminal and juvenile justice systems. The answers to these questions, we suggest, are somewhat discouraging. Despite repeated past failures, modern-day justice systems continue to treat crime primarily as an individual-level phenomenon.

Blame is assessed and punishments assigned in the hope that retribution will achieve deterrence. As the evidence mounts, however, more and more voices are demanding that a new look be taken at traditional methods of controlling crime, criminal offenders, and criminogenic environments. These voices direct attention to social forces external to the system, toward communities, families, and other means of informal control. Prospects for change appear to be promising and scientifically justified as new forms of social control emerge to challenge the state's "monopoly on justice." Hope lies in the emergence of new and informed *partnerships* that can address juvenile delinquency at multiple levels of intervention.

NOTES

1. We do not subscribe entirely to the thesis advanced by Zimring and Hawkins (1997) that lethal violence, rather than crime, is "the problem." However, it is the more serious forms of crime and delinquency, including violent crime, which we believe should be the primary focus of justice agencies.

2. The first was popularly known as the Wickersham Commission, after its distinguished chairman, former U.S. Attorney General George W. Wickersham. The second, Commission on Law Enforcement and the Administration of Justice, was created by executive order of President Lyndon Johnson in 1965.

3. Ohlin noted that few experimental programs or careful research evaluations existed at the time of the 1960s crime commission (1975, pp. 109–10).

4. Excellent summaries of this literature are provided in the collaborative work of Farrington and Welsh (2006) and Welsh and Farrington (2006).

5. Some confusion exists regarding the "root causes" of crime and delinquent behavior. In his Foreword to Farrington and Welsh (2007), James Q. Wilson argues that "most of the root causes of crime are not . . . social issues" such as high unemployment and poor schools "but deeply ingrained features of the human personality and its early experiences" (Wilson, 2007, p. v). Macro-level conditions are also "root causes" and are in all likelihood causally related to the individual-level risks of crime and delinquent behavior identified in both the etiological and the experimental literature.

6. Detached workers were adults who worked with youth gangs on the street rather than primarily in traditional youth-serving building-centered programs.

7. This research was designed primarily for theory testing and development and did not include systematic evaluation of intervention effects (see Short & Strodtbeck, 1965/1974).

8. Citations of research have been removed from this quotation.

7 | WHAT IS THE WORLD COMING TO? (AND WHAT DOES IT HAVE TO DO WITH JUVENILE DELINQUENCY?)

> The collapse of Western culture first became obvious in the 1920s.
> C. John Sommerville (1990, p. 272)

The rise and decline of civilizations is a topic of endless fascination and speculation. Many scholars, and even more pundits, have attempted to document and explain what has happened, what is happening, and what may happen. What seemed "obvious" to Sommerville (above) has been a source of despair for some and encouragement—even inspiration—for others. "Family values," for example, once embraced patriarchal control and subservience of wives and children to the whims and dictates of male heads of households. Change has both positive and negative effects, depending on one's point of view.

THE NATURE OF SOCIAL CHANGE

It is in the nature of social change that some things change more rapidly than others. Material culture (technology, for example) changes much more rapidly than do such elements of nonmaterial culture as beliefs and values and the social organizations and institutions that are based on them. Beliefs and values do change, of course, and social inventions such as juvenile court and police systems came about, in part, as adaptations to such changes. Unfettered authority of parents over their children changed only gradually before juvenile courts assumed some of that authority. Later, as we have seen, the authority of juvenile courts to intervene in the lives of parents and their children was constrained by the U.S. Supreme Court based on constitutional civil rights criteria.

Social and cultural changes occur for many reasons. In recent centuries, change has accelerated as scientific discoveries and technologies based on them have rapidly accumulated. Economic institutions changed, for example, when technologies associated with the industrial revolution brought on factory production methods and later made possible mass production of goods. Although the factory system furthered the exploitation of children in the form of child labor, gains in production later made possible the education of children on a broader scale as factory manufacturing became more efficient and demanded a more skilled and educated labor force.[1] The latter half of the twentieth century witnessed a revolution in technologies of communication and transportation that continues unabated, with no end in sight.

The implications of many changes for child rearing and for control of delinquent behavior are far from clear. On the one hand, young people adapt more quickly to some changes, especially technological changes, than do their elders. Surveys also find that young people fear social change much less than others. These findings quite likely are causally related. That is, young people are less fearful of social change in some measure because of their familiarity with and favorable response to technological change. They not only adapt readily to it, in many cases they are its creators. They develop it, use it, and market it. However, although such changes make youth more vital to some institutions, especially economic institutions, they may also further isolate youth from other institutions, and they may force young people to bear responsibilities for which they are unprepared and ill-equipped.

SOMETHING NEW HAS BEEN ADDED

In some respects, the gap between generations that was noted in Chapter 5 has grown wider, and youth culture in many varieties has diffused throughout much of the world. As if to make an already complex and cumbersome system even more so, technological and other changes have hugely altered the nature of many economic, political, and social relationships. These changes pose special problems for child saving and for systems of juvenile and criminal justice.

Many changes result from what has been called "globalization." Although scholars debate precisely what is happening, no one doubts that the ways in which economic and political affairs are conducted throughout the world have changed in many ways. Of particular concern to the subject of this book, the technologies that make possible instant communication also facilitate the diffusion of fads and fashions associated with youth culture, including youth gang culture. Those fashions sometimes are associated with the darker side of international conflict and sectarian strife. A March 24, 2005 USA Today headline proclaimed, "Ex-child soldier now Kenya's hottest rapper." This apparent good news was offset by another that described the "Tragic challenge of child soldiers." What do we know about such matters?

Over the past decade, sociologist John Hagedorn and other social scientists have studied global changes and their significance for young people. Although the primary focus of this work has been on youth gangs, the theme developed applies more broadly to many children in many places. The economy that was shaped by the industrial revolution has been replaced by economies and societies dominated by "network" and "information" technologies, disrupting many traditional social and economic relationships and making possible others. Adaptations to these changes include the coalescing of some traditional street gangs around powerful *resistance* ideologies based on fundamentalist religious and nationalist identities and economic crime. Evidence of these identities is found in the hip-hop culture and "gangsta rap" in the United States and many other countries. Examples of street gangs that have been transformed into entrepreneurial gangs with international ties to drug cartels and organized political activity (both in support of and in opposition to the status quo) have been well documented by gang researchers over many years. Chicago's notorious El Rukns, for example, were transformed from a small south-side street gang in the late 1950s (the Blackstone Rangers), to the Black P. Stone Nation, and later to a criminal organization willing to engage in terrorist activity against the United States. There is good evidence that gang culture has spread to Central and South America as a result of the U.S. policy of deporting thousands of immigrants with criminal records. It is clear, as well, that the Internet has played an important role in the activities of some street gangs and has become an important tool for both terrorist groups and their opponents.

Sociologist Jack Goldstone argues that "Al Qaeda is like gangs in U.S. cities or social protest movements throughout the world" in that poverty (and conditions associated with poverty) motivates opposition to "perceived injustices" and participation in behaviors that provide "short-term rewards" despite obvious risk and danger (2002, p. 151).

Data concerning the effects on children of sectarian and other conflicts remain at a very primitive level, and systematic study is nonexistent. Only recently have systematic efforts begun to document the role of organized forms of violence in young people's lives, and how and why children become involved in violence in such varied contexts as

Brazilian *favelas*, death squads and vigilantism in South Africa, child soldiers in Sierra Leone, Colombia, and Sri Lanka, protection rackets in Nigeria, and the export of gang culture from Los Angeles and other U.S. cities to other countries. Although we need to know much more about the conditions giving rise to these forms of child exploitation and behavior, such problems clearly require more than merely local attention if they are to be adequately addressed.

BUT, AREN'T ALL YOUTH PROBLEMS, LIKE POLITICS, *LOCAL*?[2]

Despite the occurrence of tumultuous events in other parts of the world, we all live our lives in *local* contexts: in families and communities, in friendship and work groups, and in other organizations. The point to the above discussion, however, is that global developments affect commerce and communication, and often erect barriers to options available to local communities. They may, for example, create both licit and illicit opportunities at the local level. Neither groups nor individuals share equally in the social, economic, and political advantages that accrue from change. Some who are bypassed by economic opportunities and feel themselves exploited and disenfranchised by existing (or changing) conditions may react in delinquent or criminal ways, individually or in groups.

Malcolm Klein's volume in this Master's Series, *Chasing After Street Gangs*, notes the apparent similarity in both macro-level and individual-level conditions of joining street gangs and becoming "boy soldiers" in civil wars (2007, p. 35). Child soldiering and involvement in local street gangs have eerily similar conditions of *risk*, including poverty, family and educational problems, and peer influences. Viewed from this perspective, problems of child saving increase both in scale and in the complexity of causal influences, and certainly in problems of control. Although we must not equate street gangs and delinquents, we all have a stake in both types of youth problems.

CHANGING PERSPECTIVES ON SOCIAL CONTROL: CHILD SAVING IN A WORLD IN TURMOIL

We have set a new record; no other people seem ever to have been so preoccupied with children.

(Mary Ellen Goodman, 1970, p. 11)

Ironically, these changes are occurring against the backdrop of acute concerns and anxieties related to child rearing and preparation of children for a world that we do not understand. A significant part of adults' preoccupation with, and anxiety about, children is related to their fears of social change and the chasm that exists between the social worlds of many adults and children. Much, in fact, is changing in the social worlds of both adults and children around the world.

Our preoccupation with children coincides with continuing debates over the future of juvenile courts, as noted in the previous chapter. It coincides as well with fundamental changes in social control that have been occurring throughout the world over the past quarter of a century or more. Private police, for example, now far outnumber municipal and other publicly-funded police, and there are many more private than public police systems. The role of government in policing increasingly "is to regulate the standards of these private security providers" (Braithwaite, 2000, p. 52). Privatization of prisons and other places of secure confinement is another growing trend, especially in the United States. Data from the most recent Census of Juveniles in Residential Placement (Table 7.1) show that although fewer juveniles were being held in public residential facilities in 2003 than in 1997, part of this drop was offset by gains made by private facilities during the same

TABLE 7.1 JUVENILE OFFENDERS IN RESIDENTIAL PLACEMENT, 2003

	Number of Juvenile Offenders			Percent Change 1997–2003		
	Type of Facility			Type of Facility		
Most Serious Offense	All	Public	Private	All	Public	Private
Total offenders	**96,655**	**66,210**	**30,321**	**−8**	**−12**	**3**
Delinquency	**91,831**	**64,662**	**27,059**	**−7**	**−12**	**11**
Person	33,197	23,499	9,671	−6	−13	21
Criminal homicide	878	803	73	−54	−56	−28
Sexual assault	7,452	4,749	2,698	34	20	68
Robbery	6,230	5,157	1,073	−33	−35	−22
Aggravated assault	7,495	5,745	1,741	−21	−24	−7
Simple assault	8,106	4,984	3,113	22	21	25
Other person	3,036	2,061	973	38	22	87
Property	26,843	18,740	8,073	−16	−18	−10
Burglary	10,399	7,481	2,904	−17	−21	−7
Theft	5,650	3,793	1,848	−22	−26	−12
Auto theft	5,572	3,756	1,812	−15	−14	−16
Arson	735	514	220	−19	−25	0
Other property	4,487	3,196	1,289	−4	−4	−6
Drug	8,002	4,851	3,137	−12	−23	15
Drug trafficking	1,810	1,284	522	−37	−41	−24
Other drug	6,192	3,567	2,615	0	−14	28
Public order	9,654	6,782	2,866	0	−5	11
Weapons	3,013	2,346	665	−28	−29	−24
Other public order	6,641	4,436	2,201	20	16	29
Technical violation	14,135	10,790	3,312	14	5	56
Status offenses	**4,824**	**1,548**	**3,262**	**−29**	**−11**	**−36**
Ungovernability	1,825	253	1,570	−36	−45	−34
Running away	997	417	577	−33	−14	−43

(continued)

| | Number of Juvenile Offenders ||| Percent Change 1997–2003 |||
| | Type of Facility ||| Type of Facility |||
Most Serious Offense	All	Public	Private	All	Public	Private
Truancy	841	207	634	−37	−49	−32
Curfew violation	203	65	138	5	−18[a]	21
Underage drinking	405	210	186	27	86	−10
Other status offense	553	396	157	−14	98	−64

[a] Percent change is based on a denominator less than 100.

Note: Total includes juvenile offenders held in tribal facilities.

Source: Adapted from Snyder & Sickmund (2006, p. 198).

period. Clearly, if this trend continues, current notions of juvenile justice are likely to change drastically, as are the government's role and responsibilities in the process.

As is the case when control responsibilities are placed into the hands of private companies and organizations, the primary government role in the *restorative and procedural justice* programs that were discussed at the close of Chapter 6 is to ensure fairness and equity in decision making and in the practice of justice. Braithwaite notes the similarities between increased citizen participation in restorative justice programs for individuals (and their families and communities) and the control of misbehavior on the part of businesses and industries.[3] The *logic* of corporate control is to bring competing entities together in "communities of fate," thereby promoting conformity with agreed-upon rules and building trust, in much the same sense that restorative justice seeks to promote trust among individuals, families, and local communities in their common interest in safety and the quality of life.

Effective control of misbehavior, whether by individuals or by corporate entities, requires fairness and commitment to the common good—conformity with standards of performance (in the case of corporations) and acceptable behavior (in the case of individuals). Standards of performance for corporations, even in highly competitive industries, have been developed both by legal and by private means, with the major role of government limited to ensuring enforcement of regulations and a level playing field. Because delinquent and criminal behavior (by individuals or groups such as street gangs) jeopardize community well-being as well as victimize those who are personally and directly affected, the restorative theory of deterrence argues that here, too, the major role of government is to serve as a backup to informal relations and processes, a last rather than first choice alternative for control.

Once again, we see that problems of social control are influenced by both local and global changes. Braithwaite and others writing in this rapidly developing field cite restorative justice efforts in schools, churches, and ethnic communities, as well as in efforts to control delinquent behavior and crime, and in "self-regulatory" programs among businesses and industries. Increasingly, it is likely that problems of social control will involve global and nongovernmental forces as well as international relationships.

Restorative justice and the development of communities of fate "involve a shift from a blame culture to a learning culture" (Braithwaite, 2005, p. 289). Human beings are unique among animal species (despite the similarity in our DNA) in our advanced human ability to use symbols. This ability, as we noted in Chapter 5, makes possible forethought and self-reflection, facilitating learning and control of our own behavior. Adam Gopnik's argument in the following quote refers to another uniquely important human quality. It is the combination of these two abilities that gives us hope for the future.

> . . . what makes people uniquely interesting is their capacity for gauging their environment and changing it; . . . the more

we measure, the more accurately we see what things are actually like.

(Adam Gopnik, 2006b, p. 59)

And so we return to the civic dimension of life, for that in the long run is the context in which both old and new problems of crime and delinquency are likely to be resolved, exacerbated, or both, as we struggle with social change and its dislocations. Social change, driven by discoveries in science and technological applications, is not going to stop. Political, economic, and social institutions surely will attempt not only to adapt to change but to direct it. Many decisions that affect our lives personally and in local communities now are made in far away places that seem beyond our control. Perhaps the best advice we can give as we close this book is "Stay tuned; and get involved!" It's your life!

NOTES

1. We recognize, of course, that such changes occurred unevenly in different societies and that the exploitation of child labor remains a serious problem in many parts of the world.
2. Thomas P. "Tip" O'Neil, longtime speaker of the U.S. House of Representatives, once famously observed that "All politics is local." A recent RAND Corporation study concludes that "All terrorism is 'local,' or at least will start locally" (Wermuth, 2004, p. 4).
3. An important context of his analysis is the "corporatization of the world," in which "most of the things done for good or ill in the world are now the acts of corporations rather than individuals" (Braithwaite, 2000, p. 57).

REFERENCES CITED IN THE TEXT

Abbott, A. 1999. *Department & discipline: Chicago sociology at one hundred*. Chicago: University of Chicago Press.

Abbott, A. 2001. *Chaos of disciplines*. Chicago: University of Chicago Press.

Agnew, R. 1992. Foundation for a general strain theory of crime and delinquency. *Criminology* 30:47–87.

Anderson, E. 1999. *Code of the streets: Decency, violence, and the moral life of the inner city*. New York: W.W. Norton and Company.

Archibold, R.C. 2007, January 17. A city's violence feeds on black-Hispanic rivalry. *New York Times*, pp. A1, A15.

Aries, P. 1962. *Centuries of childhood: A social history of family life* (R. Baldick, Trans.). New York: Vintage Books.

Bandura, A. 1986. *Social foundations of thought and action: A social cognitive theory*. Englewood Cliffs, NJ: Prentice-Hall.

Bernard, T.J. (ed.). 2006. *Serious delinquency: An anthology*. Los Angeles: Roxbury.

Blumstein, A., Cohen, J., Roth, J.A., and Visher, C.A. (eds.). 1986. *Criminal careers and career criminals*. Washington, D.C.: National Academy Press.

Braithwaite, J. 1989. *Crime, shame and reintegration*. New York: Cambridge University Press.

Braithwaite, J. 2000. The new regulatory state and the transformation of criminology. In *Criminology and social theory*, edited by D. Garland and R. Sparks, pp. 47–69. New York: Oxford University Press.

Braithwaite, J. 2002. *Restorative justice and responsive regulation*. New York: Oxford University Press.

Braithwaite, J. 2005. Between proportionality & impunity: Confrontation–truth–prevention. *Criminology* 43:283–306.

Breed v. Jones, 421 U.S. 519 (1975).

Bremner, R.H. (ed.). 1970–74. *Children and youth in America: A documentary history* (vols. 1–3). Cambridge, MA: Harvard University Press.

Brooks, D. 2006, May 25. Of love and money. *New York Times*, p. A27.

Brown, R.M. 1979. Historical patterns of American violence. In *Violence in America: Historical & comparative perspectives*, edited by H.D. Graham and T.R. Gurr (rev. ed.), pp. 19–48. Beverly Hills: Sage.

Bureau of Labor Statistics. 2006. *National Longitudinal Survey of Youth 1997* (machine-readable files). Washington, D.C.: U.S. Department of Labor, Bureau of Labor Statistics. http://www.bls.gov/nls (visited December 20, 2006).

Bursik, R.J., Jr. 2000. The systematic theory of neighborhood crime rates. In *Of crime and criminality: The use of theory in everyday life*, edited by S.S. Simpson, pp. 87–103. Thousand Oaks, CA: Pine Forge Press.

Bursik, R.J., Jr. 2002. The systemic model of gang behavior: A reconsideration. In *Gangs in America III*, edited by C.R. Huff, pp. 71–82. Thousand Oaks, CA: Sage.

Bursik, R.J., Jr., and Grasmick, H.G. 1993. *Neighborhoods and crime: The dimensions of effective community control.* Lexington, MA: Lexington Books.

Cahill, T. 1995. *How the Irish saved civilization: The untold story of Ireland's heroic role from the fall of Rome to the rise of Medieval Europe.* New York: Doubleday.

Clear, T.R., Cole, G.F., and Reisig, M.D. 2006. *American corrections* (7th ed.). Belmont, CA: Wadsworth Publishing.

Cohen, S. 1985. *Visions of social control: Crime, punishment, and classification.* Cambridge, UK: Polity Press.

DeMause, L. 1973. The history of childhood: The basis for psychohistory. *History of Childhood Quarterly* 1, no. 1:1–3.

DiIulio, J.J., Jr. 1996. *How to stop the coming crime wave.* New York: Manhattan Institute.

Eddings v. Oklahoma, 455 U.S. 104 (1982).

Esbensen, F-A. 2004. Evaluating G.R.E.A.T.: A school-based gang prevention program. *Research for Policy* (NCJ 198604). Washington, D.C.: U.S. Department of Justice, Office of Justice Programs, National Institute of Justice.

Farrington, D.P. 2003. Developmental and life-course criminology: Key theoretical and empirical issues—The 2002 Sutherland Award Address. *Criminology* 41:221–256.

Farrington, D.P., and Welsh, B.C. 2006. A half century of randomized experiments on crime and justice. *Crime and Justice* 34:55–132.

Farrington, D.P., and Welsh, B.C. 2007. *Saving children from a life of crime.* Oxford, UK: Oxford University Press.

Federal Bureau of Investigation. 1961, 1965, 1970, 1975, 1980, 1990, 1995, 2000, 2005. Crime in the United States. *Uniform Crime Reporting Program.* Washington, D.C.: Department of Justice, Federal Bureau of Investigation.

Federal Bureau of Investigation. 2003. Age-specific arrest rates and race-specific arrest rates for selected offenses, 1993–2001. *Uniform Crime Reporting Program.* Washington, D.C.: Department of Justice, Federal Bureau of Investigation.

Federal Bureau of Investigation. 2005. Crime in the United States 2005. *Uniform Crime Reporting Program.* Washington, D.C.: Department of Justice, Federal Bureau of Investigation.

Feld, B.C. 1999. *Bad kids: Race and the transformation of the juvenile court.* New York: Oxford University Press.

Felson, M.K. 1998. *Crime and everyday life* (2nd ed.). Thousand Oaks, CA: Pine Forge Press.

Geffen, E.M. 1978. Violence in Philadelphia in the 1840s and 1850s. In *Riot, rout, and tumult: Readings in American social and political violence,* edited by R. Lane and J.J. Turner, Jr., pp. 112–132. Westport, CT: Greenwood Press.

Germany, K.B. 2007. War on poverty. http://faculty.virginia.edu/sixties/readings/War%20on%20Poverty%20entry%20Poverty%20Encyclopedia.pdf (visited March 21, 2007).

Glaser, D. 1971. *Social deviance.* Chicago: Markham.

Goldstone, J.A. 2002. States, terrorists, and the clash of civilizations. In *Understanding September 11,* edited by C. Calhoun, P. Price, and A. Timmer, pp. 139–158. New York: Social Science Research Council.

Goodman, M.E. 1970. *The culture of childhood: Child's-eye views of society and culture.* New York: Teachers College Press.

Gopnik, A. 2006a, June 5. Headless horseman: The Reign of Terror revisited. *The New Yorker,* pp. 80–84.

Gopnik, A. 2006b, October 23. Rewriting nature. *The New Yorker,* pp. 50–59.

Hakeem, M. 1957–58. A critique of the psychiatric approach to the prevention of juvenile delinquency. *Social Problems* 5, no. 3:194–205.

Hirschi, T., and Selvin, H.C. 1967. *Delinquency research: An appraisal of analytic methods.* New York: Free Press.

Horowitz, R. 1983. *Honor and the American dream: Culture and identity in a Chicano community.* New Brunswick, NJ: Rutgers University Press.

Howell, J.C. 2006. [Review of *Our children, their children: Confronting racial and ethnic differences in American juvenile justice*]. *Social Service Review* 80:750–753.

Hughes, L.A., and Short, J.F., Jr. 2005. Disputes involving youth street gang members: Micro-social contexts. *Criminology* 43, no. 1:43–76.

Hughes, L.A., and Short, J.F., Jr. 2007. *The duality of the code of the streets: Why it matters.* Unpublished manuscript, University of Nebraska at Omaha.

In re Gault, 387 U.S. 1 (1967).

In re Winship, 397 U.S. 358 (1970).

Jacobs, M.D. 1990. *Screwing the system and making it work.* Chicago: University of Chicago Press.

Kent v. United States, 383 U.S. 541 (1966).

Klein, M.W. 2007. *Chasing after street gangs: A forty-year journey.* Upper Saddle River, NJ: Prentice-Hall.

Lane, R. 1969. Urbanization and criminal violence in the 19th century: Massachusetts as a test case. In *Violence in America: Historical and comparative perspectives,* edited by H. Graham and T. Gurr, pp. 359–370. Washington, D.C.: U.S. Government Printing Office.

Laub, J.H., and Sampson, R.J. 2003. *Shared beginnings, divergent lives: Delinquent boys to age 70.* Cambridge: Harvard University Press.

Lerman, P. (ed.). 1970. *Delinquency and social policy.* New York: Praeger.

Lipsey, M.W., Wilson, D.B., and Cothern, L. 2000. Effective intervention for serious juvenile offenders. *Juvenile Justice Bulletin* (NCJ 181201). Washington, D.C.: U.S. Department of Justice, Office of Justice Programs, Office of Juvenile Justice and Delinquency Prevention.

Maxson, C.L., and Klein, M.W. 1997. *Responding to troubled youth.* New York: Oxford University Press.

McKeiver v. Pennsylvania, 403 U.S. 528 (1971).

Merton, R.K. 1957. *Social theory and social structure* (rev. and enlarged ed.). New York: Free Press of Glencoe.

Messner, S.F., and Rosenfeld, R. 2007. *Crime and the American Dream* (4th ed.). Belmont, CA: Wadsworth Publishing.

Miczek, K.A., Haney, M., Tidey, J., Vivian, J., and Weerts, E. 1994. Neurochemistry and pharmacotherapeutic management of aggression and violence. In *Understanding and preventing violence: Biobehavioral influences,* edited by A.J. Reiss, K.A. Miczek, and J.A. Roth, vol. 2, pp. 245–515. Washington D.C.: National Academy Press.

Moffitt, T.E. 1993. Life-course-persistent and adolescence-limited antisocial behavior: A developmental taxonomy. *Psychological Review* 100:674–701.

Mosher, C.J., Miethe, T.D., and Phillips, D.M. 2002. *The mismeasure of crime.* Thousand Oaks, CA: Sage.

Ohlin, L.E. 1975. Report on the President's Commission on Law Enforcement and Administration of Justice. In *Sociology and public policy: The case of presidential commissions,* edited by M. Komarovsky, pp. 93–115. New York: Elsevier.

Pastore, A.L., and Maguire, K. (eds.). 2006. *Sourcebook of criminal justice statistics* (Online). http://www.albany.edu/sourcebook (visited January 15, 2007).

Petrosino, A., Turpin-Petrosino, C., and Buehler, J. 2007. Scared straight and other juvenile awareness programs. In *Preventing crime: What works for children, offenders, victims, and places,* edited by B.C. Welsh and D.P. Farrington, pp. 87–101. Dordrecht, The Netherlands: Springer.

Platt, A.M. 1969. *The child savers: The invention of delinquency.* Chicago: University of Chicago Press.

President's Commission on Law Enforcement and Administration of Justice. 1967. *Task Force Report: Juvenile Delinquency and Youth Crime.* Washington, D.C.: U.S. Government Printing Office.

Reiss, A.J., Jr., and Roth, J.A. (eds.). 1993. *Understanding and preventing violence.* 4 vols. Panel on the Understanding and Control of Violent Behavior, National Research Council. Washington, D.C.: National Academy Press.

Roper v. Simmons, 543 U.S. 551 (2005).

Rothman, D.J. 1971. *The discovery of the asylum: Social order and disorder in the New Republic.* Boston: Little, Brown and Co.

Sampson, R.J. 2002. Transcending tradition: New directions in community research, Chicago style. *Criminology* 40:213–230.

Sampson, R.J., Morenoff, J.D., and Earls, F. 1999. Beyond social capital: Spatial dynamics of collective efficacy for children. *American Sociological Review* 64:633–660.

Sarri, R.C., and Hasenfeld, Y. (eds.). 1976. Brought to justice? Juveniles, courts, and the law. *National Assessment of Juvenile Corrections.* Ann Arbor: University of Michigan.

Schall v. Martin, 467 U.S. 253 (1984).

Schlossman, S.L. 1977. *Love and the American delinquent: The theory and practice of "progressive" juvenile justice, 1825–1920.* Chicago: University of Chicago Press.

Schwartz, G. 1987. *Beyond conformity or rebellion: Youth and authority in America.* Chicago: University of Chicago Press.

Shaw, C.R., and McKay, H.D. (1969[1942]). *Juvenile delinquency and urban areas* (rev. ed.). Chicago: University of Chicago Press.

Short, J.F., Jr. 1990. *Delinquency and society.* Englewood Cliffs, NJ: Prentice-Hall.

Short, J.F., Jr. 1998. The level of explanation problem revisited—The American Society of Criminology 1997 Presidential Address. *Criminology* 36:3–36.

Short, J.F., Jr., and Strodtbeck, F.L. (1965/1974). *Group process and gang delinquency.* Chicago: University of Chicago Press.

Silver, A. 1967. The demand for order in civil society: A review of some themes in the history of urban crime, police, and riot. In *The police: Six sociological essays,* edited by D. Bordua, pp. 1–24. New York: Wiley & Sons.

Smith v. Daily Mail Publishing Co., 443 U.S. 97 (1979).

Snyder, H.N., and Sickmund, M. 2006. *Juvenile offenders and victims: 2006 national report.* Washington, D.C.: U.S. Department of Justice, Office of Justice Programs, Office of Juvenile Justice and Delinquency Prevention.

Sommerville, C.J. 1990. *The rise and fall of childhood*. New York: Vintage Books.

Stahl, A.L., Puzzanchera, C., Sladky, A., Finnegan, T.A., Tierney, N., and Snyder, H.N. 2005. *Juvenile Court Statistics 2001–2002*. Washington, D.C.: U.S. Department of Justice, Office of Justice Programs, Office of Juvenile Justice and Delinquency Prevention, National Center for Juvenile Justice.

Stanford v. Kentucky, 492 U.S. 361 (1989).

Stapleton, W.V., and Teitelbaum, L.E. 1972. *In defense of youth: A study of the role of counsel in American juvenile courts*. New York: Russell Sage.

Sullivan, W. 1986. *Reconstructing public philosophy*. Berkeley: University of California Press.

Sullivan, M.L. 1989. *"Getting paid": Youth crime and work in the inner city*. Ithaca, NY: Cornell University Press.

Task Force on Juvenile Delinquency. 1967. *Report on juvenile justice and consultants' papers*. Washington D.C.: The President's Commission on Law Enforcement and Administration of Justice 1967.

Thompson v. Oklahoma, 487 U.S. 815 (1988).

Tittle, C.R., and Villemez, W.J. 1977. Social class and criminality. *Social Forces* 56, no. 2:474–502.

Tittle, C.R., Villemez, W.J., and Smith, D.A. 1978. The myth of social class and criminality: An empirical assessment of the empirical evidence. *American Sociological Review* 43, no. 5: 643–656.

Urban Institute. 2006. Child welfare and well-being: Building a 21st century system for kids. *Thursday's Child*. http://www.about.chapinhall.org/conferences/urban/jun2006/conference.html (visited February 20, 2007).

Wade, R. 1969. Violence in the cities: A historical view. Reprinted in *Riot, rout, and tumult: Readings in American social and political violence*, edited by R. Lane and J. Turner, Jr., pp. 349–363. Westport CT: Greenwood Press.

Welsh, B.C., and Farrington, D.P. (eds.). 2006. *Preventing crime: What works for children, offenders, victims, and places*. Dordrecht, The Netherlands: Springer.

Wermuth, M.A. 2004. *Empowering state and local emergency preparedness: Recommendations of the Advisory Panel to Assess Domestic Response Capabilities for Terrorism Involving Weapons of Mass Destruction*. Santa Monica, CA: RAND Corporation.

Wilkins v. Missouri, 492 U.S. 361 (1989).

Wilson, W.J. 1987. *The truly disadvantaged: The inner city, the underclass, and public policy*. Chicago: University of Chicago Press.

Wilson, J.Q. 2007. Foreword to *Saving children from a life of crime*, edited by David P. Farrington and Brandon C. Welsh. Oxford, UK: Oxford University Press.

Zimring, F.E., and Hawkins, G. 1997. *Crime is not the problem: Lethal violence in America*. New York: Oxford University Press.

BIBLIOGRAPHY

Author's note: There is a vast literature on juvenile delinquency and delinquents, and on social change. From that literature, the following sources were especially helpful as this book was written:

Anderson, M., Kaufman, J., Simon, T.R., Barrios, L., Paulozzi, L. Ryan, G., Hammond, R., Modzeleski, W., Feucht, T., Potter, L., and the School-Associated Violent Deaths Study Group. 2001. School-associated violent deaths in the United States, 1994–1999. *Journal of the American Medical Association* 286, no. 21: 2695–2702.

Baldassare, M. (ed.). 1994. *The Los Angeles riots: Lessons for the urban future.* Boulder: Westview.

Ball-Rokeach, S., and Short, J.F., Jr. 1985. Collective violence: The redress of grievance and public policy. In *American violence and public policy,* edited by L.A. Curtis, pp. 155–180. New Haven: Yale University Press.

Bayley, D. 1983. Police history. In *Encyclopedia of crime and justice,* edited by S.H. Kadish, pp. 1120–1125. New York: Free Press.

Beckett, K., and Sasson, T. 2003. *The politics of injustice: Crime and punishment in America.* Thousand Oaks, CA: Sage Publications.

Bernard, T.J. 1992. *The cycle of juvenile justice.* New York: Oxford University Press.

Bilchik, S. 2000. Self-reported delinquency by 12-year-olds, 1997. *Fact Sheet* (FS–200003). Washington, D.C.: U.S. Department of Justice, Office of Justice Programs, Office of Juvenile Justice and Delinquency Prevention.

Bortner, M.A. 1982. *Inside a juvenile court: The tarnished ideal of individualized justice.* New York: New York University Press.

Braithwaite, J. 1989. The myth of social class and criminality reconsidered. *American Sociological Review* 46:36–57.

Brett, R., and Specht, I. 2004. *Young soldiers: Why they choose to fight.* Boulder, CO: Lynne Rienner.

Bureau of Justice Assistance. 1994. Understanding community policing: A framework for action. *Monograph* (NCJ 148457). Washington, D.C.: U.S. Department of Justice, Office of Justice Programs, Bureau of Justice Assistance.

Butts, J.A., and Mears, D.P. 2001. Reviving juvenile justice in a get-tough era. *Youth and Society* 33, no. 2:189–194.

Butts, J.A., Buck, J., and Coggershall, M.B. 2002. The impact of teen court on young offenders. *Research Report.* Washington, D.C.: The Urban Institute.

Chesney-Lind, M., and Shelden, R.G. 2003. *Girls, delinquency, and juvenile justice* (3rd ed.). Belmont, CA: Wadsworth Publishing.

Cicourel, A. 1968. *The social organization of juvenile justice.* New York: Wiley.

Cullen, F.T. 1994. Social support as an organizing concept for criminology: Presidential address to the Academy of Criminal Justice Sciences. *Justice Quarterly* 11, no. 4: 527–559.

Denning, D. 2002. Is cyber terror next? In *Understanding September 11,* edited by C. Calhoun, P. Price, and A. Timmer, pp. 191–197. New York: Social Science Research Council.

Elliott, D.S., Ageton, S.S., Huizinga, D., Knowles, B.A., and Canter, R.J. 1983. The prevalence and incidence of delinquent behavior, 1976–1980: National estimates of delinquent behavior by sex, race, social class, and other selected variables. *National Youth Survey Report No. 26.* Boulder, CO: Behavioral Research Institute.

Emerson, R. 1977. *Judging delinquents.* Chicago: Aldine.

Empey, L.T., and Stafford, M.C. 1991. *American delinquency: Its meaning and construction* (3rd ed.). Belmont, CA: Wadsworth Publishing.

Farrington, D.P., Jolliffe, D., Hawkins, J.D., Catalano, R.F., Hill, K.G., and Kosterman, R. 2003. Comparing delinquency careers in court records and self-reports. *Criminology* 41(3):933–958.

Federal Bureau of Investigation. 2006. About the UCR program. http://www.fbi.gov/ucr/05cius/about/about_ucr.html (visited October 2, 2006).

Feld, B.C. 1999. The honest politician's guide to juvenile justice. *The Annals of the American Academy of Political and Social Sciences* 564:10–27.

Fritsch, E.J., Caetti, T.J., and Hemmons, C. 1996. Spare the needle but not the punishment: The incarceration of waived youth in Texas prisons. *Crime and Delinquency* 42, no. 4: 593–609.

Gramckow, H.P., and Tompkins, E. 1999. Enabling prosecutors to address drug, gang, and youth violence. *Juvenile Accountability Incentives Block Grant Program* (NCJ 178917). Washington, D.C.: U.S. Department of Justice, Office of Justice Programs, Office of Juvenile Justice and Delinquency Prevention. http://www. ncjrs. gov/ html/ ojjdp/ jjbul9912-2/ contents. html (visited March 7, 2007).

Groeneveld, L.P., Short, J.F., Jr., and Thoits, P.A. 1979. *Design of a study to assess the impact of income maintenance on delinquency.* Final Report prepared for the Law Enforcement Assistance Administration, Department of Justice. Menlo Park, CA: SRI International, Menlo Park, California.

Hagedorn, J.M. 2006a. *Gangs in the global city.* Champaign, IL: University of Illinois Press.

Hagedorn, J.M. 2006b. The global impact of gangs. In *Studying youth gangs,* edited by J.F. Short, Jr., and L.A. Hughes, pp. 181–192. Lanham, MD: AltaMira Press.

Hartney, C. 2006. Youth under age 18 in the adult criminal justice system. *Fact Sheet, Views from the National Council on Crime and Delinquency.* Oakland, CA: National Council on Crime and Delinquency.

Hawkins, D.F. (ed.). 1995. *Ethnicity, race, and crime: Perspectives across time and place.* Albany, NY: SUNY Press.

Hsia, H.M., Bridges, G.S., and McHale, R. 2004. Disproportionate minority confinement 2002 update. *OJJDP Summary* (NCJ 201240). Washington, D.C.: U.S. Department of Justice, Office of Justice Programs, Office of Juvenile Justice and Delinquency Prevention.

Klein, M.W. 1969. Gang cohesiveness, delinquency, and a street-work program. *Journal of Research in Crime and Delinquency* 6:135–166.

Klein, M.W. 1971. *Street gangs and street workers.* Englewood Cliffs, NJ: Prentice-Hall.

Krisberg, B. 2005. *Juvenile justice: Redeeming our children.* Thousand Oaks, CA: Sage Publications.

Landesco, J. 1929. *Organized crime in Chicago: Part III of The Illinois Crime Survey 1929.* Chicago: University of Chicago Press.

Lane, R. 1967. *Policing the city: Boston, 1822–1885.* Cambridge, MA: Harvard University Press.

Lengermann, P., and Neibrugge-Brantley, J. 2006. Thrice told: Narratives of sociology's relation to social work. In *Sociology in America,* edited by C. Calhoun, pp. 63–114. Chicago: University of Chicago Press.

Lynch, J.P. 2002. Trends in juvenile violent offending: An analysis of victim survey data. *Juvenile Justice Bulletin* (NCJ 191052). U.S. Department of Justice, Office of Justice Programs, Office of Juvenile Justice and Delinquency Prevention.

Mahoney, A.R. 1987. *Juvenile justice in context.* Boston: Northeastern University Press.

Makkai, T., and Braithwaite, J. 1994. Reintegrative shaming and compliance with regulatory standards. *Criminology* 32:361–385.

Manning, P.K., and Von Maanen, J. (eds.). 1978. *Policing: A view from the street.* Santa Monica, CA: Goodyear Publishing.

Matza, D. 1964. *Delinquency and drift.* New York: Wiley.

National Crime Victimization Survey. 2006. *Criminal victimization in the United States, 2005 statistical tables.* Washington, D.C.: U.S. Department of Justice, Office of Justice Programs, Bureau of Justice Statistics.

National Criminal Justice Association. 1997. Juvenile justice reform initiatives in the states: 1994–1996. *Program Report* (NCJ 165697). Washington, D.C.: U.S. Department of Justice, Office of Justice Programs, Office of Juvenile Justice and Delinquency Prevention.

National Institute of Justice. 2006. Drug courts: The second decade. *NIJ Special Report* (NCJ 211081) Washington, D.C.: U.S. Department of Justice, Office of Justice Programs, National Institute of Justice.

National Juvenile Court Data Archive. 2006. History of the Archive. *National Center for Juvenile Justice.* Pittsburgh, PA. http://ojjdp.ncjrs.org/ojstatbb/njcda/asp/history.asp (visited September 2, 2006).

Nettler, G. 1985. Social class and crime, one more time. *Social Forces* 63, no. 4: 1076–1077.

Nimick, E.H., Snyder, H.N., Sullivan, D.P., and Tierney, N.J. 1985. *Juvenile court statistics, 1983.* Pittsburgh, PA: National Center for Juvenile Justice.

Ogburn, W.F. 1922. *Social change, with respect to culture and original nature.* New York: Huebsch.

OJJDP Statistical Briefing Book. 2006. Juvenile court cases. National Juvenile Court Data Archive. National Center for Juvenile Justice. Pittsburgh, PA. http://ojjdp.ncjrs.gov/ojstatbb/court/qa06201.asp?qaDate=2003 (visited December 22, 2006).

Parent, D., Dunworth, T., McDonald, D., and Rhodes, W. 1997. Key legislative issues in criminal justice: Transferring serious juvenile offenders to adult courts. *Research in Action* (NCJ 161840). Washington, D.C.: U.S. Department of Justice, Office of Justice Programs, National Institute of Justice.

Pepinsky, H.E., and Quinney, R. (eds.). 1991. *Criminology as peacemaking.* Bloomington, IN: Indiana University Press.

Piaget, J. 1965. *The moral judgment of the child* (M. Gabain, Trans.). New York: Free Press.

Puzzanchera, C., Stahl, A.L., Finnegan, T.A., Tierney, N., and Snyder, H.N. 2004. *Juvenile Court Statistics 2000.* Washington, D.C.: U.S. Department of Justice, Office of Justice Programs, Office of Juvenile Justice and Delinquency Prevention, National Center for Juvenile Justice.

Rand, M.R. 2005, February. The National Crime Victimization Survey: 32 Years of measuring crime in the United States. Paper presented at the meeting of the Siena Group on Social Statistics, Helsinki.

Rennison, C.M. 2002. Hispanic victims of violent crime, 1993–2000. *Special Report* (NCJ 191208). Washington, D.C.: U.S. Department of Justice, Office of Justice Programs, Bureau of Justice Statistics.

Sampson, R.J. 1985. Neighborhood and crime: The structural determinants of personal victimization. *Journal of Research in Crime and Delinquency* 22, no. 1:7–40.

Sampson, R.J. 1987. Urban black violence: The effect of male joblessness and family disruption. *American Journal of Sociology* 93, no. 2:348–382.

Sampson, R.J., Raudenbush, S.W., and Earls, F. 1997. Neighborhoods and violent crime: A multilevel study of collective efficacy. *Science* 277:918–924.

Sherman, L.W. 1993. Defiance, deterrence, and irrelevance: A theory of the criminal sanction. *Journal of Research in Crime and Delinquency* 30:445–473.

Sherman, L.W. 2003. Reason for emotion: Reinventing justice with theories, innovations, and research—The American Society of Criminology 2002 Presidential Address. *Criminology* 41:1–38.

Sherman, L.W. 2005. The use and usefulness of criminology, 1751–2005: Enlightened justice and its failures. *Annals of the American Academy of Political and Social Science* 600:115–135.

Short, J.F., Jr. (ed.). 1971. *The social fabric of the metropolis: Contributions of the Chicago school of urban sociology.* Chicago: University of Chicago Press.

Short, J.F., Jr., and Hughes, L.A. (eds.). 2006. Moving gang research forward. In *Studying youth gangs,* edited by J.F. Short, Jr. and L.A. Hughes, pp. 225–238. Lanham, MD: AltaMira Press.

Steffensmeier, D., and Harer, M.D. 1991. Did crime rise or fall during the Reagan presidency? The effects of an "aging" U.S. population on the nation's crime rate. *Journal of Research in Crime and Delinquency* 28, no. 3:330–359.

Steffensmeier, D., Zhong, H., Ackerman, J., Schwartz, J., and Agha, S. 2006. Gender gap trends for violent crimes, 1980 to 2003: A UCR-NCVS comparison. *Feminist Criminology* 1, no. 1:72–98.

Strom, K.J. 2000. Profile of state prisoners under age 18, 1985–97. *BJS Special Report* (NCJ 176989). Washington, D.C.: U.S. Department of Justice, Office of Justice Statistics, Bureau of Justice Statistics.

Tittle, C.R. 1983. Social class and criminal behavior: A critique of the theoretical foundation. *Social Forces* 62, no. 2:334–358.

Tittle, C.R. 1985. A plea for open minds, one more time: Response to Nettler. *Social Forces* 63, no. 4:1078–1080.

Tittle, C.R., and Meier, R.F. 1990. Specifying the SES/delinquency relationship. *Criminology* 28, no. 2:271–299.

Tittle, C.R., Villemez, W.J., and Smith, D.A. 1982. One step forward, two steps back: More on the class/criminality controversy. *American Sociological Review* 47:435–438.

Tonry, M.H. (ed.). 1997. *Ethnicity, crime, and immigration: Comparative and cross-national perspectives.* Chicago: University of Chicago Press.

Uniform Crime Reporting Program. 2006. *Crime in the United States 2005.* Washington, D.C.: U.S. Department of Justice, Federal Bureau of Investigation.

Walker, S.E. 1977. *A critical history of police reform: The emergence of professionalism.* Lexington, MA: Lexington Books.

Walker, S.E., Spohn, C., and DeLone, M. 2004. *Color of justice: Race, ethnicity, and crime in America* (4th ed.). Belmont, CA: Wadsworth Publishing.

Wilson, W.J. 1996. *When work disappears: The world of the new urban poor.* New York: Knopf.

Winner, L., Lanza-Kaduce, L., Bishop, D.M., and Frazier, C.E. 1997. The transfer of juveniles to criminal court: Reexamining recidivism over the long term. *Crime and Delinquency* 43, no. 4:548–563.

INDEX

A
Abbott, A., 91, 105–106
Adolescence, 99–104
"Adolescent-limited" offender. *See* Juvenile delinquency (juvenile delinquents)
Age, parental and state control, 12–13
Age and delinquency. *See* Juvenile delinquency (juvenile delinquents)
Agnew, R., 89
Al Qaeda. *See* Terrorism (and Al Qaeda, etc.)
America, colonial, 8–13
American Dream, 88–90
Anderson, E., 101, 118
Anti-Drug Abuse Act (1986), 36
"Antisocial potential", 87
Archibold, R.C., 74
Aries, P., 5

B
Baby boomers, 99–100
Bandura, A., 97
Bernard, T.J., 38, 119
Black P. Stone Nation, Blackstone Rangers, 130
Boston, 10–11
Braithwaite, J., 107, 117, 123, 124–125, 132, 134–135
  See also Restorative justice
Breed v. Jones (1975). *See* Supreme Court, U.S.
Bremner, R.H., 9–10
Britain (British), 8, 10
Brooks, D., 92–93
Brown, R.M., 10
Buehler, J., 113
Bureau of Alcohol, Tobacco, Firearms and Explosives, 44
Bureau of Justice Statistics (BJS), 41, 42, 45
Bureau of Labor Statistics, 41, 44
Bursik, R.J., 91–92

C
Cahill, T., 18
Capital, human and social, 93–96
Catholic Church, 7
Census Bureau, 41, 45
Census of Juveniles in Residential Placement. *See* Prison
Chicago, 72
Chicago Area Project (CAP). *See* Social control
Chicago school, 30
Child, children, childhood, 2
  history of, 6–8
  as little adults, 5
  treatment and indifference toward, 6
Child abuse and neglect, 2, 17, 20
Child rearing (practices and concerns), 1–17
  See also Social change
Children, exploitation of (child soldiers, death squads, *favelas*). *See* Social change
Citizens (civic dimension, engagement), 2, 121, 136
Civil rights movement, 25, 29
Class. *See* Social class
Clear, T.R., 19, 37
Cocaine (crack/powdered). *See* "Get tough" era and policies
"Code of the street", 101–102
  and gangs, 102
  See also Anderson, E.
Cohen, S., 125
Cole, G.F., 19, 37
Collective efficacy, 94–96
Columbine High School, 55, 104
Community. *See* Juvenile delinquency (juvenile delinquents)
Context (contextualization)
  defined, 3
  history as, 3
Cothern, L., 114–115
Crime
  and morality, 11, 12
  and sin, 8
Criminal justice system. *See* Juvenile justice system
Criminal law, 14

147

Cultural differentiation. *See* Subculture
Culture, Western
    and family values, 127

D

"Dark figure of crime", 47
    See also Data, types of
Data, types of
    official records (UCR, police, courts), 41–42, 45–47
    self-reports, 43–44, 47
    strengths and weaknesses, 45–48
    and triangulation, 48
    victimization, 44, 47
Death penalty. *See* Supreme Court, U.S.
Delinquency, delinquent behavior, delinquents. *See* Juvenile delinquency (juvenile delinquents)
DeMause, L., 6
Detached workers (street workers). *See* Social control
Developmental and life course perspectives, 85–88
Differential association, 105
DiIulio, J.J., 67
Disproportionate Minority Confinement (DMC). *See* Juvenile justice system

E

Earls, F., 93–94, 118
Ecology, systemic model, 91. *See* Juvenile delinquency (juvenile delinquents)
Eddings v.Oklahoma (1975). *See* Supreme Court, U.S.
El Rukns. *See* Black P. Stone Nation, Blackstone Rangers
Esbensen, F-A., 114
Europe, 7–8

F

Family (families)
    functions of, 5
    government power, 7–8
    See also Juvenile delinquency (juvenile delinquents)
"Family values", 127
Farrington, D.P., 81, 85–87, 116–117, 123
Federal Bureau of Investigation (FBI), 41–42
Feld, B.C., 33
Felson, M.K., 75
Firearms, 102–104
Fortas, A. *See* Supreme Court, U.S.

G

Gang/gang culture. *See* Social change; Subculture
Gang Resistance Education and Training (GREAT), 44
    See also Social control
Gangs and delinquency. *See* Juvenile delinquency (juvenile delinquents)
Gault, In re (1966). *See* Supreme Court, U.S.
Geffen, E.M., 11
Gender and delinquency. *See* Juvenile delinquency (juvenile delinquents)
Germany, K.B., 30
"Get tough" era and policies, 20, 32–35, 65
    and crack cocaine and the "War on Drugs", 35–37
    and waiver to criminal court, 33–34
Glaser, D., 99
Globalization. *See* Social change
Goldstone, J.A., 130
Goodman, M.E., 132
Gopnik, A., 1, 135–136
Grasmick, H.G., 91
Guns. *See* Firearms

H

Hagedorn, J.M., 129
Hakeem, M., 20
Hasenfeld, Y., 120
Hawkins, G., 126
"Hierarchy rule", 46–47
    See also Data, types of
"Hippie" life styles, 25
Hirschi, T., 77, 78
History, why we study, 1
Horowitz, R., 106
House of Refuge (New York), 12
Howell, J.C., 122
Hughes, L.A., 102, 118
Human capital. *See* Capital, human and social

I

Industrial Revolution. *See* Social change
Institutional anomie. *See* Theory, theoretical perspectives
Institutions, as contexts, 4
International Association of Chiefs of Police (IACP), 42

J

Jacobs, M.D., 120–122
"Jim Crow" laws, 65

Johnson, L.B., 29
Johnson, L.B., and the "War on Poverty", 29–30
Juvenile court(s), 3, 15
   abuses and violations of rights, 19
   advent of, 39, 128
   as" back-up institutions", 120
   ask environment of, 15
   challenges to, 21–22
   effectiveness, 122
   evolution of, 19–38
   and the federal government, 29–30
   invention of, 3–4
   jurisdictional variation, 2, 20
   movement, 16–17
   and police, 20
   responsibilities of, 2
   and separation from criminal courts, 25
   See also Data, types of
Juvenile delinquency (juvenile delinquents) and age, 55–58
   arrests and arrest rates (UCR), 49–50, 59
   and conventional institutions (family and school), 54–55, 78–79, 97–98, 102–103
   court records, 50–52
   defined, 1–2
   and delinquent peers, 78
   distribution of (categoric risks, correlates, empirical regularities), 49–75
   early statutes, 20
   and ecology (urban, suburban, rural), 72–74
   explanation of, 77–106
   and gangs, 73–74
   and gender, 58–63
   as ideas, behavior, and social problems, 1–5, 13, 16
   and individual traits, 79–80, 81, 96–97
   measurement of, 19–38
   prevention and control. *See* Social control
   and race/ethnicity, 63–67
   recidivism, 111–112
   and residential placement, 132–134
   self-reports, 52–54
   serious, consequences of, 107
   and social class, 71–72
   specialization *v.* versatility, 104
   status offenses and offenders, 30–32, 52, 107
   taxonomy of ("adolescent-limited" *v.* "life-course persistent"), 104
   victimization data, 54
   See also Data, types of
Juvenile Justice and Delinquency Prevention Act (JJDPA), 18, 31, 52
Juvenile justice system
   and the criminal justice system, 107–108
   cycle of, 119–120
   and the federal government, 110
   historical origins and advent of, 13–15, 107
   and the police, 12
   and race disparities and Disproportionate Minority Confinement (DMC), 33, 35–36, 38
   and residential placement, 32
   state monopoly of, 126
   See also Juvenile court(s); Prison and residential placement

K

Kennedy, J.F., 29
Kent v. United States (1966). *See* Supreme Court, U.S.
Klein, M.W., 31–32, 99, 131

L

Lane, R., 11–12
Laub, J., 106
Law (law enforcement), 4
   See also Juvenile justice system, and the police
Lerman, P., 9, 12
Levels of explanation. *See* Theory, theoretical perspectives
"Life-course persistent" offender. *See* Juvenile delinquency (juvenile delinquents)
Life course perspectives. *See* Developmental and life course perspectives
Lipsey, M.W., 114–115
London, 9–11
Los Angeles, 73

M

Massachusetts Bay Colony, 8–9
Maxson, C.L., 31–32
McKay, H.D., 72, 84, 90, 108
McKeiver v. Pennsylvania (1971). *See* Supreme Court, U.S.

Merton, R.K., 88–89
Messner, S.F., 89–90
Miczek, K.A., 86
Middle Ages, 5
Miethe, T.D., 39
Moffitt, T.E., 104
Monitoring the Future (MTF),
    44, 53, 63, 67
  See also Juvenile delinquency
    (juvenile delinquents), self-reports
Moral panic (and "innocent youth
    fallacy"), 75
Morals (morality), 11–12, 95
Morenoff, J.D., 93–94, 118
Mosher, C.J., 39, 40

N

National Center for Chronic Disease
    Prevention and Health
    Promotion, 44
National Center for Juvenile Justice
    (NCJJ), 42, 50
  See also Juvenile delinquency (juvenile
    delinquents), court records
National Center of Health, 41
National Council of Juvenile and Family
    Court Judges, 42
National Crime Victimization Survey
    (NCVS)/National Crime Survey
    (NCS), 45, 47, 63, 67
  See also Juvenile delinquency (juvenile
    delinquents), victimization data
National Incident-Based Reporting System
    (NIBRS), 42
National Juvenile Court Data Archive
    (NJCDA), 42
National Legal Aid and Defender
    Association, 37
National Longitudinal Study of
    Adolescent Health, 44
National Longitudinal Survey of Youth
    1997 (NLSY97), 44, 53, 63, 67
  See also Juvenile delinquency (juvenile
    delinquents), self-reports
National Research Council, 81
National Sheriffs' Association (NSA), 42
National Youth Survey (NYS)/National
    Youth Survey Family Study
    (NYSFS), 44
Nation states, emergence of, 7
Networks. *See* Social networks
New York, 11–12
  See also House of Refuge (New York)

O

Office of Juvenile Justice and Delinquency
    Prevention (OJJDP), 31
Official records. *See* Data, types of
  See also Juvenile delinquency (juvenile
    delinquents)
Ohlin, L.E., 109–110
O'Neil, T.P., 136

P

Parens patriae, 18, 28, 50
  See also Supreme Court, U.S.
Parents (parental control), 12–13, 17, 128
Petrosino, A., 113
Philadelphia, 11
Phillips, D.M., 39
Physical sciences, 39
Police, 4, 11–12, 14–15, 102, 120, 128
  community, 38
  and juvenile court(s), 20
  and professionalization, 20
  See also Privatization
Powers, E., 9
President's Commission on Law
    Enforcement and Administration
    of Justice, 25, 45, 108
  Task Force on Juvenile Delinquency,
    16, 31
President's Committee on Juvenile
    Delinquency and Youth Crime, 30
Prison and residential placement
  adult, 13
  Census of Juveniles in Residential
    Placement, 51–52, 132–134
  juveniles in, 34–35
  See also Juvenile justice system;
    Privatization
Privatization, 132–134
  and government's role, 134
Project on Human Development in Chicago
    Neighborhoods, 44, 93, 117–118

R

Race/ethnicity and delinquency.
  See Juvenile delinquency
    (juvenile delinquents)
Recidivism. *See* Juvenile delinquency
    (juvenile delinquents)
Reformatories, 13, 14
Reisig, M.D., 19, 37
Religion(s) (doctrines)
  and children, 7
  and government, 7

Residential placement. *See* Juvenile justice system
  See also Juvenile delinquency (juvenile delinquents); prison and residential placement
Restorative justice. *See* Social control
Revolution (revolutionary war), 10
Roper v. Simmons (2005). *See* Supreme Court, U.S.
Rosenfeld, R., 89–90
Rothman, D.J., 12

S

Sampson, R.J., 93–94, 117–118
Sarri, R.C., 120
Scared Straight. *See* Social control
School and juvenile delinquency. *See* Juvenile delinquency (juvenile delinquents)
Schools, as gatekeepers, 14–15
Schwartz, G., 94, 101
Science and technology, 6, 39
  See social sciences
Self-control, 97
Self-reports. *See* Data, types of
  See also Juvenile delinquency (juvenile delinquents)
Selvin, H.C., 77, 78
Sentencing Commission, U.S., 37
Shaw, C.R., 72, 84, 90, 108–109
Short, J.F., 102, 118
Sickmund, M., 111–112
Smith, D.A., 71
Smith v. Daily Mail Publishing Co. (1979). *See* Supreme Court, U.S.
Snyder, H.N., 111–112
Social capital. *See* Capital, human and social
Social change, 2–3
  and child-rearing, 128
  and exploitation of (child soldiers, death squads, *favelas*), 130–131
  and gangs, gang culture, youth culture, 129–131
  and globalization, 129
  and the Industrial Revolution, 128–129
  and local concerns and problems, 131–132
  the nature of, 127–129
  and social control, 132
  and technology, 39, 127–130
  See also Juvenile court(s)

Social class, 5, 8, 14
  See also Juvenile delinquency (juvenile delinquents)
Social control, 107–126
  cognitive behavioral therapy (CBT), 113–114
  Community Action Program (CAP), 109, 123
  detached workers (street workers), 102, 118–119, 123
  Drug Abuse and Resistance Education (DARE), 113
  Gang Resistance Education and Training (GREAT), 113
  income maintenance experiments (Denver and Seattle), 117
  levels of intervention, 114–119
  and the "no-fault society", 120–123
  restorative justice, 124–125, 134–135
  Scared Straight, 112–113
  teen court, 113
  See also Juvenile justice system; Social change
Social disorganization. *See* Theory, theoretical perspectives
Social movements and the juvenile justice system, 13–14
Social networks, 91–94
Social sciences, 3, 39
  movement, 13
Social service agencies, 14–15
Sommerville, C.J., 6, 7–8, 127
"Staging areas", 101
Stanford v. Kentucky (1989). *See* Supreme Court, U.S.
Stapleton, W.V., 27
Status offenders and reformatories, 13
  See also Juvenile delinquency (juvenile delinquents)
Stewart, P. *See* Supreme Court, U.S.
Strain. *See* Theory, theoretical perspectives
Strodtbeck, F.L., 126
Subculture, 98–102
  gang/gang culture, 99, 102
  and status and stratification, 100
  youth, 99–102
Sullivan, M.L., 100
"Superpredators", 67–70
Supplementary Homicide Reports, 63
  See also Federal Bureau of Investigation (FBI)

INDEX **151**

Supreme Court, U.S., 19, 26–29, 37–38, 128
  Breed v. Jones (1975), 29
  and the death penalty, 37–38
  Eddings v. Oklahoma (1982), 37
  In re Gault (1966), 26–27, 109
  In re Winship (1970), 29
  Justice A. Fortas, 27
  Justice P. Stewart, 28
  Kent v. United States (1966), 26–27
  McKeiver v. Pennsylvania (1971), 28
  and *parens patriae*, 28
  Roper v. Simmons (2005), 37
  Smith v. Daily Mail Publishing Co. (1979), 38
  Stanford v. Kentucky (1989), 38
  Thompson v. Oklahoma (1988), 37
  Wilkins v. Missouri (1989), 38
  See also "Get tough" era and policies

T

Task Force on Juvenile Delinquency. *See* President's Commission on Law Enforcement and Administration of Justice
Teitelbaum, L.E., 27
Terrorism (and Al Qaeda, etc.), 130
Theory, theoretical perspectives and crime and delinquency, 105
  levels of explanation, 80–85, 104–105
  social disorganization, 90
  strain and institutional anomie, 88–90
  systemic model of human ecology, 91
  versus. description, 77–80
  See also Developmental and life course perspectives; juvenile delinquency (juvenile delinquents)
Thompson v. Oklahoma (1988). *See* Supreme Court, U.S.
Tittle, C.R., 71
Triangulation. *See* Data, types of
Turpin-Petrosino, C., 113

U

"Underclass", 74
Uniform Crime Reports (UCR), 59, 66
  See also Data, types of; juvenile delinquency (juvenile delinquents)
United States of America (USA), 8
Urban Institute, The, 51

V

Victimization data. *See* Data, types of
  See also Juvenile delinquency (juvenile delinquents)
Viet Nam War, 25, 29
Villemez, W.J., 71
Violence and U.S. history, 10
Virginia Company, 9–10
Virginia Polytechnic Institute and State University, 104

W

Waiver to criminal court. *See* "Get tough" era and policies
"War on Drugs." *See* "Get tough" era and policies
"War on Poverty." *See* Johnson, L.B.
Welsh, B.C., 81, 116–117, 123
Wickersham, G. W. (Commission), 126
Wilkins v. Missouri (1989). *See* Supreme Court, U.S.
Wilson, D.B., 114–115
Wilson, J.Q., 141
Wilson, W.J., 74
Winship, In re (1970). *See* Supreme Court, U.S.

Y

Youth Risk Behavior Surveillance Survey, 44

Z

Zimring, F.E., 126